BUILDING

SUCCESSFUL

RELATIONSHIPS

MICHAEL FLETCHER

BUILDING

SUCCESSFUL

RELATIONSHIPS

7 Keys to Winning & Keeping the Hearts of Others

Published by Manna Imprint.

Italicized words in Scripture passages represent the author's emphasis.

Editing by Katharine Floro.

Layout & design by James Richardson & Anna Wiggins.

ISBN-13: 978-0-9976960-0-4

Printed in the United States of America.

20 19 18 17 16   2 3 4

CONTENTS

INTRODUCTION

You picked this book up for a reason. Something about winning or keeping the heart of another person attracted your attention. You might want to strengthen an already great marriage, or mend a damaged one. Perhaps you're grieving the loss of a friendship or pining over the departure of a wayward child. You could be looking for ways to strengthen or expand your client base. Maybe you're just searching for a friend. Whether your concern is establishing new relationships in the future, fixing broken ones from the past, or making your present ones stronger, you've come to the right place. When you finish this book, you'll have the tools you need to do all three! Your healthy relationships will be stronger; you will be on a new path to restore the broken ones; and you'll know how to establish new relationships that really last.

ALL OF LIFE
IS ABOUT RELATIONSHIPS

Every person comes into the world through a relationship. That relationship may be broken before the person is born, but it took some sort of connection between two people to produce a child. Before that child knows anything about life, he is already wrapped up in relationships that will affect his future in dramatic ways. Whether the father is present and in love with the child's mother or is absent and estranged from her will have a bearing on the course of the child's life. If the doctors and nurses who participate in his birth are experiencing stress from personal relationships on the brink of collapse, his quality of care may be affected.

This little fellow has no control over these circumstances. But as he grows, he gains a greater say in the relationships that surround his life. And relationships are everywhere! Parents, grandparents, friends, teachers, and classmates govern his early childhood. Counselors, girlfriends (watch out!), coaches, teammates, enemies, rivals, and professors shape his youth. Relationships with his spouse, children, in-laws, bosses, clients, business contacts, old friends, new friends, used-to-be friends—all these fill and influence his life. If he is going to be successful in life, he'll have to be successful in relationships! And the same applies to you and me.

If we're going to be successful in life, we'll have to be successful in relationships!

THE QUALITY OF OUR RELATIONSHIPS DIRECTLY AFFECTS THE QUALITY OF LIFE WE ENJOY

All my life I have heard people speak of success in terms of money in the bank. The thought is that the greater the bank balance, the higher the quality of life a person enjoys; but in the course of over thirty years of ministry, I've learned that this is one of life's great deceptions.

One of the most successful doctors in our city once requested an appointment with me. As he waited for me in the lobby of our office suite (what goes around comes around), people recognized him as a well-respected member of the medical community and one of the more financially successful physicians in the region. He had the money in the bank; he had the reputation; he was the portrait of success. But inside he was a broken and desperate mess! His marriage was secretly—but soon to be not-so-secretly—falling apart. He opened up to a friend, who sent him to me, and now he sat slowly decomposing in front of me as he shared his tragic story. He could have used the relational truths contained in this book ten years earlier. In all seven areas that I will cover, he had fallen short and his marriage was an apt portrayal of the results.

Interestly, back in the lobby several other people were also waiting for appointments with members of my staff. None of them had the kind of investment account this doctor had. None of them drove a car as expensive as his. But all of them were infinitely happier in their relationships than he was. Who would you say enjoyed the better quality of life?

Am I saying that you can't have money and happiness? Not at all! I know plenty of wealthy people who enjoy life tremendously. What I'm saying is that money doesn't determine your quality of life. The most important things in life are not defined in terms of dollars and cents, but in terms of people. The people in our lives (or absent from them) powerfully impact our happiness and in large measure determine our quality of life.

You probably didn't need to read this book to know that. You have already experienced the power and the pain of this truth. There have been times when all troubles seemed to fade away because you looked across the room and forgot everything but him; you knew he was the One. Or your teenage daughter stepped into your room just before heading off to bed to tell you how much she appreciated all you do for her and what a great mother you have been. You smiled and thanked her, but you couldn't sleep because of the joy and the realization that all your hard work and heartache was worth it.

There have also been times when you saw your "best friend" out on the town with another friend for the third time in a row. You remember the sorrow of realizing that although they were your best friend, you weren't theirs. You felt so foolish for not seeing it sooner! Perhaps you woke up one morning and finally faced the fact that you no longer really knew the person whose head was on the pillow beside you. Lying there in painful silence, you couldn't remember when the downward slide began or how it started, but you knew you were at the bottom; you knew the spark was dead.

We've all experienced success and failure in relationships. The tragedy is that most of us don't know what made for that success or failure. Why do some relationships thrive while others die? Is there a rhyme or reason to the relationship game? Yes, I believe there is! I believe that one key universal truth with seven applications determines the future of every relationship. A bold statement, isn't it? Read on and see: the fact is that a closer examination of your successes and failures will reveal the same thing. I didn't just wake up with this idea one fine morning. It's a truth that has come to light through my study of the Scriptures, God's handbook for life, and which I have observed in action in the lives of thousands of people over the years.

SO WHY DID YOU PICK UP THIS BOOK?

What was it about winning or keeping the heart of another that caught your eye? Are you interested in making new friends? Are you trying to bolster a struggling marriage? Are you concerned about your connection to your sons and daughters? Are you lonely for companionship, or looking for a boost in your business relationships to propel you over the edge of financial success? Get ready! The adventure is about to begin. Be forewarned: at some point you're going to say, "No way, this is too easy!" But give these ideas a try and you will see that they really do work.

ONE PROFOUND TRUTH

Keep your heart with all diligence, for out of it spring the issues of life.

Proverbs 4:23 (NKJV)

The New International Version of the Bible translates Proverbs 4:23 as follows: "Above all else, guard your heart, for it is the wellspring of life." Either way, it is a simple but very profound verse. The four ideas contained here can revolutionize your life.

THE CENTER OF LIFE

First, we find out that at the center of life resides the heart. The heart spoken of here is not the physical pump that runs our circulatory system; it is what makes us human. Biblical theologians define it as "the governing organ of the soul," and Jesus Himself said that everything that flows out of a person's mouth finds its origin in the heart.[1] Our day-to-day language reflects this idea in a thousand ways. When we are profoundly disappointed or sad, we say, "It broke my heart." When we marry someone, we may say, "I give you my heart." When we fall in love we might say, "He stole my heart." When we desperately want something, we say, "I have my heart set on it." We know instinctively that the heart is the most important part of us.

GIVING YOUR HEART AWAY

Second, we are told to keep or guard our hearts. The reason is obvious—the heart is easily captured by other people. When that happens we put ourselves into another person's hands.

When a mother holds her newborn for the first time, she instantly gives her heart away. The look on her face is worth more than money can buy. I have seen it eight times, each time one of my children came into the world. In that moment my wife Laura was able to set aside all the pain of the hours that preceded, because something—someone—had captured her heart. Her face took on a glow as she tenderly stroked the face of a tiny new Fletcher. Each time I had to fight back tears as I recognized a bond that was instant, permanent, and holy—something that existed only between the two of them.

---

[1] See Matthew 12:34.

It happened because my wife gave her heart away immediately and without reservation.

I saw that same look on the face of the wife of one of my staff members during a movie. Unbeknownst to them, we snuck into a seat right behind them after the previews. In the middle of the action, I saw her turn and just look up at the face of her husband, totally oblivious to the film. Her expression said, *I have given my heart completely to you, and that decision has brought me into a place of security and joy. I am totally satisfied that I will belong to you and you only for the rest of my life.* Life can only truly be lived when our hearts are in the hands of others. Giving our hearts away is the key to happiness.

But the admonition in Proverbs to "guard" is there for a reason. Giving our hearts to others also puts us in a position to experience pain. I've seen that pain on the faces of many people and have experienced it myself. When we give our heart to another, we give them a piece of ourselves—and not just any piece, but the most important one. That's why we're often hurt the most by those we love. Love opens us up to them and them to us. The more open and vulnerable we become—the more we give our hearts away—the more potential for joy and intimacy as well as sorrow and pain.

If that were the end of the story, life would be easy. We would simply make a careful study of prospective friends and lovers and only give our hearts to the most trustworthy among them. Our experience tells us that life works differently. All of us have had somebody unexpected worm their way into our hearts. Many a romance begins with the tale of a persistent pursuer, who, at first resisted, continued the chase. The lovers laugh as they reminisce—*I never thought, who would have known...*

Proverbs 4:23 warns us to "guard" because our hearts are so easily subject to theft. C.S. Lewis said it best:

> There is no safe investment. To love at all is to be vulnerable. Love anything, and your heart will certainly be wrung and possibly be broken. If you want to make sure of keeping it intact, you must give your heart to no one, not even to an animal. Wrap it carefully round with hobbies and little luxuries; avoid all entanglements; lock it up safe in the casket or coffin of your selfishness. But in that casket...it will become unbreakable, impenetrable, irredeemable. The only place outside Heaven where you can be perfectly safe from all the dangers and perturbations of love is Hell.[2]

In heaven we are safe from the dangers of love, because love is perfect; in hell, because love is absent. In this life, however, we are always subject to the theft of our hearts. Once love has taken hold, the object of that love is in control. Our plans, our goals, our entire lives all change. Well-thought-out decisions come into question, all because of love.

My father said no more animals—emphatically and definitely. He was deaf to our cries and pleading. No more pets! All that ended when we brought that little kitten home. Dad

---

[2] C.S. Lewis, *The Four Loves* (New York: Harcourt, Brace, 1960), 121.

started off with, "We cannot keep that thing. Why did you bring this cat home?" Moments later it became, "Only for tonight—but after you clean it up, it has got to go!" By the next morning, he was saying, "Now, I am not going to be responsible for taking care of that cat!" You know the drill; once he saw it and gave it a little time, the little furry bundle who could not speak our language was getting a portion of my father's income in vet bills and food!

WHOEVER HAS YOUR HEART HAS YOUR LIFE

The third—and perhaps most valuable—idea we mine from Proverbs 4:23 is that all of life springs forth from the heart. Treat this insight like treasure: whoever has your heart has your life. No more profound truth could be spoken about human relationships than that. This is the key to present and future happiness, and the explanation of past and present pain. If you only underline one thing in this book, underline this: *whoever has your heart has your life.*

Over the years I have had far too many occasions to witness the transference of a child's allegiance from their parents to their peers, often with tragic consequences. When children are young they depend on their parents for almost everything. Sometimes as they grow, they undergo a shift from parent dependency to peer dependency. There is nothing wrong with children making friends (in fact, they won't be healthy without friends), but friendship and peer dependency are two different things.

How does this happen? Simple: the parents lost the heart of their child. Some friend or group of friends has the heart of the child now, and things begin to change. The values the son or daughter grew up with begin to be challenged. Next comes the establishment of new authorities. No more going to Mom and Dad for advice; the new friends are the consultants for life now. Fights between parent and child become more volatile and frequent.

Children of all ages can build strong, vibrant friendships and still enjoy a healthy relationship with their parents. There is room in the heart for everyone. But when parents lose their child's heart, that child will go looking for a place to give it. In the situation above, they found some willing takers in their friends. Does this have to happen? No way!

The same thing happens in many struggling marriages. Allen knows something is missing in his marriage, but he can't put his finger on it. When he asks Allison if everything is okay with her, she gives vague answers. Suspicion grows, and so do rumors of an affair with Allen's best friend. Finally, one day in the heat of battle, he confronts her. Stunned, she says nothing—but her face says it all. How did this happen? Weeks later Allen sits incredulously in the counselor's office. Allison says it wasn't about sex, and the counselor agrees. They say it became sexual. What happened? Somewhere along the line, without realizing it, Allen stopped nurturing her heart, and he never noticed that she was beginning to give it to someone else. When Allen's best friend had

Whoever has your heart has your life.

her heart, he had her life—sex and all. What could Allen have done differently?

We have to guard the heart, because whoever has the heart has the life. In every relationship you now enjoy—your friendships, your marriage, your children, your status as Aunt Beth's favorite niece—you won the heart of that person.

KEEPING THE HEARTS OF OTHERS

The trouble is, once we win someone's heart, we often do not continue in the pattern we started. Usually that's because we don't know what we did to win that heart in the first place! Instead we take life as it comes and wonder why some of our relationships work and some do not. We can't see a rhyme or reason to it. We look across the street in amazement; what did our neighbors do to have such great teenagers, when ours want nothing to do with us? After a string of lost friendships or years of loneliness, we wonder if there is something wrong with us. It's not us. It's our application of this simple but profound truth: the things you do to keep a person's heart are the very same things you did to win it.

What were those things, you may ask? We'll get to that soon.

THE MOST IMPORTANT THING

The fourth and final important idea outlined in Proverbs 4:23 is that we should apply diligence to this business of nurturing and guarding the heart—and not just diligence, but *all diligence*. The NIV uses the phrase "above all else". In other words, *this is the most important thing!* To enjoy life, we need a wide range of skills, but our relational skills are the most crucial. We need to become experts at winning and keeping the hearts of others. Our happiness depends on it, because our relationships depend on it.

So let's get busy. No question about it: this is going to require time and energy, and lots of both. Like all of us, you'll find old habits you'll have to change, and change is never easy. I can promise you this, however: change in this area of life will yield tremendous blessings and benefits.

I have found over the years that there are seven powerful keys we can use to open the hearts of others. Some or all of these keys were in use when you first won another's heart:

LOVE

Loving others without condition

• • •

FAITH

Believing more for someone
than they do for themselves

• • •

INTEREST

Valuing what others value

• • •

AVAILABILITY

Making room for others in crisis

• • •

RESPECT

Establishing a person's worth

TIME
The key to unlocking a heart

• • •

COMMUNICATION
The lifeline of every relationship

If you're going to keep the hearts you've won, you can't afford to lose your keys. As we move forward, you'll see more clearly how these keys work and how you can creatively use them.

LOVE

LOVING OTHERS
WITHOUT CONDITION

For God so loved the world that he gave his one and only Son, that whoever believes in him shall not perish but have eternal life.

John 3:16

In 1984, rock-and-roll icon Tina Turner released her most popular hit: "What's love got to do with it? What's love, but a second-hand emotion?...Who needs a heart when a heart can be broken?"[1] The song later served as the theme of a movie based on Tina's story of surviving an abusive marriage. Her experience of love isn't one any of us aspire to share; many of us have already encountered that pain first-

---

[1] Terry Britten & Graham Lyle, *What's Love Got to Do With it* (Capital Records, 1984).

hand, and we've had our fill. We want to live happy lives, full of relationships that will be good for the long haul, but love has brought us nothing but heartache. Like Tina, we're tempted to ask: what's love got to do with it?

WE NEED TO DECIDE ON OUR DEFINITION OF LOVE

If love is only an emotion, then Tina was right. We would be fools to put our hearts into the hands of anyone driven solely by the excitement of the moment. Love based on emotions is bound to last only as long as that emotion, and we all know that emotions can change in an instant. What nightmare could be worse than pinning all your dreams, everything about you that matters most, on the whim of someone else?

Many of us have made that fateful mistake. We entered into a relationship based on how we felt at the time. Both sides started out at the same relative level of emotion, but eventually one started to grow colder. At first we tried to hold on to what we felt was fading away. Then perhaps we tried playing it cool too, only to find out that the other person was glad we were starting to allow for a little distance. As the crack in our once-close relationship spread wider and wider, the real pain started to set in, until we found ourselves farther from our friend or lover than we had been at the beginning.

Thankfully, Tina was wrong. Love is not a "second-hand emotion". Love produces emotions, but we frequently confuse the emotional products of love with love itself. Many people chase the emotion, not realizing that they are sowing the seeds of destruction into the foundation of their relationship. They wind up building on the wrong thing—on the emotion of love, and not on the sure foundation that true love provides.

When we focus on the emotional side of love, our goal is to keep the emotion going. We like it. It makes us feel good. Very quickly we become dependent on it, as if it were a drug. When that emotion is flowing through our veins, we have a new perspective. Old burdens seem light. New problems look more like opportunities; together, we tell ourselves, we can lick anything. We are high on life, because we are high on the emotion of love—but that emotion, like all emotions, is fleeting. Unless we build something more permanent into the foundation of our relationship, we'll have nothing to land on when the high is over.

The emotions of love are wondrous—don't misunderstand me. I have been happily married to the same special woman since 1979. Not only do I love her, but I am *in love* with her. A world without that emotion would be boring. But we have to keep the horse in front of the cart. True love produces the emotion of love, but the emotion is not the end of the story. When the emotion has faded or flown, true love will still be there.

> Love based on emotions is bound to last only as long as that emotion.

But if true love is not an emotion, how should we define it?

INFATUATION

"I have loved him from the first day I saw him in class!" "I loved my third grade teacher!" "I loved Paul McCartney!" This kind of "love" is infatuation. Basically, infatuation is being in love with the idea of being in love. For those who have fallen into it, infatuation looks a lot like love, and discerning the difference from the inside can be difficult. But the two are miles apart. Infatuation focuses on how another makes you feel and the benefit you receive from being with them. A high school girl feels like more than just a high school girl when she's on the arm of a college boy. A guy jumps way up the ladder of popularity when the head cheerleader accepts his invitation to the prom. He steps up another couple of rungs if he can be seen with her the next day or so, and several more if he gets her to wear his ring.

In the end, infatuation is about me and what I am getting from this relationship, so it is inherently selfish. Much like building a relationship on the emotion of love, infatuation is flawed from the start and will doom anything you try to construct on it.

LUST

"If you loved me you would…" has been the doorway to many a disaster. How many young adults, caught up in the emotion of the moment, have confused their hormones with love and fallen into the trap? Lust is the polar opposite of love. Being inherently self-centered, it is never satisfied; like an addiction, it constantly demands new levels of excitement. As soon as one thrill becomes routine, lust throws it away in search of a new high.

Paul and Cindy loved each other deeply, or so she thought. He'd never known anyone like her. He couldn't keep his hands off her; and since they were going to get married anyway, why should he? The sex was great! They couldn't wait for the wedding; it could only get better, right? But after they were married, the guilt settled in on her. The excitement of having to sneak around was gone, and it became old hat for him. Finally, Paul found others with whom he could satisfy his misplaced passion. It was forbidden, and he was excited once more. One adulterous relationship led to another, and eventually Cindy found out. Today they are divorced. No relationship can stand on a foundation of lust, because lust can never be satisfied.

NEED-LOVE

Need-love, as C.S. Lewis terms it in *The Four Loves*, is the kind of love that everyone has for the people who care for them in the beginning of life. A baby loves her mother because her mother feeds and cares for her. That process of nurturing breeds an atmosphere of security where trust and dependency are developed. The baby feels safe; all her needs are being met. As the child matures, so does her love, until Mom is loved as much for who she is as for what she provides.

But sometimes love doesn't mature as it should, and many people try to build lasting relationships on need-love—with tragic results. *I meet your needs and you meet mine,* they think.

That sounds great, but what happens if I stop meeting your needs? Will you still love me? Or do you love me because I meet your needs? Your love for me, then, is conditioned upon what I do for you. If I ever stop meeting your needs, you will stop loving me, and our relationship will be over. So many relationships are built this way, especially in families. Some parents give or withhold love based on the performance of their child: if the child obeys, the love flows freely, but if the child rebels love is withheld. Love should never be a reward for good behavior. It should be a gift a child receives from a parent, regardless of their behavior. When parents relate to their children based on their behavior, they communicate to their children that love is conditional and must be earned.

TRUE LOVE CENTERS ON UNCONDITIONAL GIVING

John 3:16 (the verse listed at the outset of this chapter) is probably the most quoted verse from the Bible, because it captures the essence of the Christian faith. But it also includes the best definition of the true character of love I have ever found: "For God so loved...that He gave..."

True love always centers on giving without regard to what we get in return. This is how God loved us, and this is how we are to love others as well.

The real trouble with love as an emotion, or infatuation, or need-love, or lust, is that they all share the same tragic flaw— each one centers on what we receive from a relationship. Each of these false forms of love tries to construct relationships on the shifting ground of self, because it fixes our eyes on what we ourselves are getting out of those relationships. Disappointed when our goals and needs go unmet, we get angry and withdraw our love in return.

THE CHURCH SHOULD MODEL CHRIST'S LOVE

There is an epidemic of confusion as to the true definition of love in the world today. Most of our past relationships have trained us to look out for number one. If a relationship doesn't meet our needs, we dump it and move on. Most people hold as a sacred truth that there is no free lunch. From our earliest days, it's ingrained in us that everyone is out for something and everything comes with conditions lodged deep in the fine print.

The Church Universal has done a pretty poor job of communicating to the world the true message of the Christian faith. We have allowed them to believe that, like their fellow human beings who expect a return for their love, God requires adherence to a certain set of laws before they can receive His love and acceptance. But God gave His Son for us with no strings attached, so that none would perish. Jesus took our penalty and removed the barrier between man and God. The message of Christianity is not rules and regulations, but love without condition.

Our church has attempted to help undo this misconception by engaging in service projects in our community designed to communicate the no-strings-attached love of God. We wash cars at no charge and refuse donations. On hot days, we give away thousands of cold drinks all over the city. We have washed toilets in area businesses and given away hot dogs and drinks at local festivals. We never ask for or accept any payment. When people ask why we would do such a thing, we tell them, "We wanted to show you that God loves you in a practical way!" Usually they shake their heads—what's the catch? What's the angle? To which we respond, "No angle, just love; nothing added, nothing required." For some people, it just won't compute.

TRUE LOVE GIVES

Let me make this very clear. True love is not oriented toward what we can get out of a relationship, but toward what we can give. True love says, "I have found in you a person I choose to love, and I am determined to demonstrate that love to you by meeting your needs, whether you meet mine or not. I give myself to you and expect nothing in return." That is true love. If we demand our love to be returned in any way, we clearly communicate that our love is conditional—and, therefore, not truly love.

Sometimes parents will respond to a rebellious child with increasing expectations that the love they have so freely given over the years be returned by at least respect from their son or daughter. That increased demand—to the parents' bewilderment—is often met by increased rebellion. But bearing in mind the definition of true love, we can understand why this happens. The love they have freely given is now being redefined as conditional in the heart and mind of their child.

The teen now thinks, "You say you love me, but you only love me so I will respect you. Fine, I'll respect you, but don't expect me to love you in return. And when I leave your home, don't look for any respect either!" Parents sometimes forget that the most powerful thing they can do is love their child despite the rebellion. Continue to touch the teen and invite him into your life. Reach for him and never give up on him, even in the midst of the storm. As Paul tells us in Romans 2:4, it is the goodness of God that leads us to repentance. Love given in the face of wrongdoing is stronger than any hostility.

TRUE LOVE INCLUDES DISCIPLINE

Of course, not everything goes in every relationship. Each relationship has its parameters, and there is a time to be tough. But when that time comes, we need to coat everything—even discipline—with love. In fact, true love includes discipline, and discipline, if properly administered, is loving. Love is sometimes firm and unbending. Love sometimes enforces an unpopular standard. Love always does what is best for another, even when they do not understand or appreciate it. Certainly, children need clear direction, and shaping them in the early years requires strong and steady discipline; but our actions toward them must always be motivated and rooted in an attitude of love.

> Love always does what is best for another, even when they don't understand or appreciate it.

PEOPLE ARE DRAWN TO THOSE WHO TRULY LOVE THEM

Albert's father died when he was very young, and his single mother did the best she could to raise him, but times were tough and so was he. Albert was supposedly a part of the youth group I led, but he hardly ever came; and when he did, he figured it was his part-time job to be aloof but disruptive. He was "cool." But when he came, I reached out to him; however unlovable he was determined to be, I was determined to love him.

One evening at home with his mother, he became belligerent to the point of violence. Fearing for the safety of the other children, his mother sent them out of the house, and not knowing what else to do she called me. By the time I got there, Albert was in a rage. My presence only made things worse—his mother had called in "the authorities"! He shouted at me—"F— God! F— the church! F— you!"—over and over. He threw iced tea at me. I stood there soaking wet and told Albert, "I don't care what you say about God, the church, or me. I love you and will continue to love you no matter what you do or where you go. And if you run from here, I'll just pray that God will raise someone up to love you in the same way." Albert did run and to my knowledge is still running, but for years he called me (once from prison) to see how things were going and to share a piece of his life. Why? Because of the power of unconditional love! People crave such love. They are irresistibly drawn to those who love them without expecting anything in return. It creates trust—not to mention the fact that you are meeting one of their most basic needs.

TRUE LOVE
CAN CHANGE A COMMUNITY

Carolynne is a middle-class lady who lives in a middle-class house and enjoys the same middle-class lifestyle as her neighbors. She doesn't have a Ph.D.; she has never written a play or recorded an album. Most people would call her average. Nevertheless, our local Human Relations Board was so impressed with her that they chose her above everyone else in our city to receive a humanitarian award for her service in Campbell Terrace.

Campbell Terrace was a housing project in our community. The people who lived there were mostly single moms and elderly women, and more than anything else they needed help in making a difference in the lives of their children. Without intervention, many of the children got sucked into a life of drugs and crime. But what were mothers to do when most of their hours were taken up trying to make ends meet? Role models were scarce. Enter Carolynne. She started a kids' club on Fridays to help teach character and provide another voice of discipline and support to the children. When she ran into needs beyond her ability to handle personally, she recruited other helpers. When she found a single mother sleeping on the floor, she tracked down someone who was giving away a bed to meet the need. Carolynne and her team did the same thing with old air conditioners and stoves, refrigerators and fans. Her example inspired men in the community to volunteer to change the oil in the cars of the residents. Every year she oversaw a project to provide Christmas presents to every mother and child in Campbell Terrace.

Carolynne didn't feel she deserved the award from the city; in fact, she was shocked she had even been considered. What had moved the city officials to honor her over the other candidates was the fact that she did all of this with no strings attached. There was nothing these people could do for her, nothing tangible they could give in return. What Carolynne had done was love them—unconditionally! She had given herself and her time to them. She had influenced them to believe that life could be different. In return, they gave her their trust, their love, and their respect. Even gang members opened their hearts to her—a middle-class white lady from Canada! In her mind, she already had her reward—she had won their hearts.

THE LOVE INSIDE YOUR CIRCLE

What kind of love exists inside the circle of your personal relationships? Are you building your relationships on the shifting sand of self by only giving according to what you expect to receive? Ask yourself the tough questions, and determine to become a giver instead. At first, the risk looks steep—what happens if no one loves you back? I am sure there will be those who take advantage of you along the way, and there will be some pain. But self-seeking love always ends in pain; that's a guarantee. In this world that constantly demands *what's in it for me*, people are looking for those who will show them genuine love. Human beings young and old will always stay close to those who give without expecting to receive.

The benefit of unconditional love is that in some way, at some time, it will always come back to us. Jesus said, "Give and it will be given to you. A good measure, pressed down, shaken together and running over, will be poured into your lap. For with the measure you use, it will be measured to you." (Luke 6:38) Don't be afraid of the risk. The more we truly give, the more we will be loved in return!

3

CHAPTER THREE

FAITH

BELIEVING MORE FOR SOMEONE
THAN THEY DO FOR THEMSELVES

But encourage one another daily, as long as it is called Today,
so that none of you may be hardened by sin's deceitfulness.

Hebrews 3:13

W hat's the best way to motivate somebody to make good choices? Warnings? Correction? Actually, according to this verse from Hebrews, it's neither of those things. Rather, we're told to "encourage one another daily." By building people up and providing positive reinforcement, we give them the power to live better lives. Of course, there is a place for warning when we see a friend setting out on a course leading to destruction, and there is a place for correction when that friend ignores the warning and crashes into the consequences of their poor decisions. But the bread-and-butter way to motivate people towards a higher level is through constant, daily encouragement.

FAITH THAT TRANSFORMS

My parents didn't just love me and my brothers and sister—they believed in us. Whatever we set our hearts on, they believed we could do it, and they told us so. They encouraged us to try new things, explore new skills—art, sports, music lessons, you name it. I even played junior varsity football at 105 pounds soaking wet with pads on! Despite their support, I still grew up—like many children—with low self-esteem. I desperately wanted to be accepted by my peers; I was afraid of being thought of as a lightweight. In my arrogant teenage perspective, the liberal arts were for lightweights; so I took every math and science class I could, planning to earn my degree in engineering.

But as time passed, I realized engineering wasn't what God had called me to; He had made me for ministry. And ministry, of course, meant liberal arts. As I sensed this new direction in my life, all my old fears of looking weak came to light. I told my pastor how terrified I was and how I wasn't cut out for the ministry. I listed all the reasons why this couldn't possibly work. "Well, then," he said, "I guess you qualify"—his unspoken point being, *ministry is not about you anyway.* Even with his encouragement, I still dreaded failure.

During the time of my ministry training, the guys I was studying alongside never told me that I would never make it; but they said it among themselves. They had reason to feel that way. I came into the group a long-haired, hippy-looking kind of guy. I was younger than the rest and extremely impetuous. I had cornered the market on pride and arrogance. To top it off, I wasn't a good speaker and showed little promise of improvement. In no way did I fit the standard pastor paradigm. I couldn't blame them for betting against me. But there were three people who didn't, and their faith was what changed my life.

BELIEF OF A WIFE

As soon as Laura, then my girlfriend and now my wife, heard that I felt called to ministry she was behind me one hundred percent. She could see it! I was amazed. She believed more for me than I did for myself. When I ran myself down in comparison to the other students and doubts and fears crept in, she was there to show me my future and set me back on course. She saw what I could and would become, and she treated me like I was already there. By this time, she already had my heart—but by having faith in me, she secured a place in my heart that no woman could take. She was more important than a girlfriend; she was a rudder and the wind in my sail. Her encouragement was a source of strength; she made me believe in myself. Invincible fortresses became sand castles as I saw myself through her eyes. She really believed I could do it! How could I live without such a person? Two and a half years later we were married. Decades later, she is still my rudder and sail.

BELIEF OF A FRIEND

Jim Laffoon, my first mentor, gave me a chance when others had no positive reinforcement to give. He talked with me about the future I hoped for—not idle talk or wishful thinking, because like Laura, Jim saw something in me that I didn't see myself. Not only was he my mentor, but he made room for me in his life as a friend. He became a safe place in the competitive world of ministerial training. Because of that, I opened up to him and let him into my heart and life. Jim's faith for me played a large role in shaping the early years of my ministry. "Michael, this is not your strongest area; you need to work on this." "Michael, your pride has blinded you to _____, and you have become judgmental." Jim saw all my crud, but with the eyes of faith, he also saw what I could become. Today, though separated by many miles, Jim is as close to me as he was then. His faith for me captured my heart and established a friendship stronger than years or distance.

BELIEF OF A PASTOR

Pastor Jerry Daley returned from a mission trip with a clear understanding that he was to move his family to Thailand and help start new churches in that country. Although he had a great staff of well-trained and competent people, Pastor Daley chose me, the youngest and least experienced of all, to be the new senior pastor of his church with 350 active members. Staff members and friends around the country quietly challenged him to think this through a little better. "The guy has potential, but at 26, with only three years of experience, do you really think he's ready? What do you see in him?" But Jerry always believed in me. From the first time I told him I felt called to ministry, he saw what I could not see in myself—and he saw it so clearly that he was prepared to put his life's work in my hands. His faith has been rewarded. As of 2016, Manna Church has grown to more than 8,600 members and has had a hand in planting more than 70 churches around the world.

Jerry's time in Thailand, however, did not go as well, and he returned home sooner than expected. Many old friends saw this as a chance to point out his faults and criticize him for his failures, but I never did; Jerry had captured my heart. By placing faith in me, he had gained my loyalty. To this day, Jerry Daley is my pastor. Over the years, due to the growth of our church and the ministries we have started, voices have encouraged me to break from the network of churches that Jerry leads and start my own. I always refuse. Why? Blind loyalty? Not at all. By demonstrating real faith in me—not just once but continually over the years— Jerry has won a place in my heart that he will always keep.

EVERYDAY CHALLENGES

Every day we face challenges to our confidence. Coworkers climbing up the corporate ladder threaten to knock us off our rung and overshadow our achievements. Children and teens constantly compare themselves to classmates and friends, almost always leaving themselves on the short end of the stick. Self-help books leave us, many times, with a clearer picture of what is wrong with us than how to make things right. Pressures from work, home and school constantly remind us of what we have to do and how far we have to go; and they draw our focus to our obvious inadequacies. The result is that our confidence erodes, and we feel unprepared to tackle the challenges ahead of us.

"Encourage" means *to give courage*. When we see more for others than they do for themselves, we literally impart courage to them. We give them the power to face the future with renewed confidence. Walls shrink into stepping stones as their perspective shifts from inadequacy to possibility, from possibility to probability. Encouragement emboldens them to see what they couldn't see before and inspires new ideas.

And as their horizons open up, so do their hearts. Trust begins to develop and love soon follows. Remember this: people are drawn to those who believe in them. When you see someone with God's eyes and speak to them from that vantage point, you give them the power to persevere. That is exactly what Laura, Jim, and Jerry did for me. Their faith for me and the potential they saw in me won my heart—and transformed my future.

THE POWER OF FAITH
TO TRANSFORM OTHERS

In his book *Bringing Out the Best in People,* Alan Loy McGinnis beautifully illustrates the transformative power of faith with a now-famous study performed by psychologist Robert Rosenthal of Harvard University and Lenore Jacobson, a San Francisco school principal. The two designed an experiment to test whether the performance of students in the classroom was impacted by the expectations of their teacher (in other words, by their teacher's faith in them). Every child in the school, from kindergarten through fifth grade, took a standardized intelligence test. The real results were not passed on to the teachers. Instead, the study administrators randomly chose names and leaked them to the teachers, leading the teachers to believe that no matter how those students presently performed in the classroom, they were in fact destined to be the cream of the crop. At the end of the year, all the students were tested again. The students whom the teachers thought were the ones with the most potential—those whose names had been "leaked"—improved their scores by 15 to 27 I.Q. points! The only thing that changed in the classroom was the expectation—that is, the faith level—of the teachers for those particular children. These children had been given courage! Someone believed in them, and that elevated them to a new level of performance.

FAITH FOR THOSE YOU LOVE

Ask yourself this: who most commonly expresses faith for your loved ones? Who believes more for them than they do for themselves? Those people are in a position to win your loved ones' hearts.

When parents begin to lose sight of the potential of their rebellious teen, they leave the door wide open for someone else—probably a friend—to see a future for their son or daughter. What future will they see? Will it be helpful or harmful? Who do we want to be the rudder for our child? It doesn't take any relational skill to see a person as they are now, but it is quite another thing to see them as they could be. Dream of your child's potential. Without trying to cast them in some specific role, picture the kind of future they are capable of having. Then—without becoming pushy—during times when your child is down and discouraged, share your vision of the wonderful life you see for them. Always believe more for them than they do for themselves. No matter what is happening today, keep your sight on a better tomorrow.

Who sees more for your spouse than they see for themselves? The boss? The cute coworker? Or you? Our loved ones need someone who will believe in them even when they fail or when others out-perform them. They need a refuge where they can receive the courage they need to face another obstacle. Whoever gives them that courage will win their hearts. Whoever continues to give them that courage will keep their hearts.

Do you want to start a new friendship, or grow one you already have? Become a person who believes in others. Begin to cultivate an image of a brighter future for those around you. Look beneath the surface and search out their potential, their hidden talents. Learn to applaud the obvious, too.

I have a close friend who has tremendous musical talent, but when he was growing up, his family worried that too much praise would make him proud. Instead they gave him none, only whispering compliments among themselves when he couldn't hear. It wasn't until he reached high school that he realized the depth of the talent that had been given him. By that time he was so filled with fear and insecurity that it took a fantastic wife, encouraging friends, and many years of healing to propel him into the success that he is today. My friend's parents could have boosted him into a greater future far sooner, but instead they chose to withhold their life-giving words.

Each of us has that same opportunity to sow encouragement and life into those around us. Everyone you know—whether they realize it or not—is hunting for people who will believe in them. Have faith for those you love. Believe more for them than they believe for themselves, and over time, you'll see their hearts open to you more and more.

CHAPTER FOUR

INTEREST
VALUING WHAT OTHERS VALUE

*Do nothing out of selfish ambition or vain conceit, but in
humility consider others better than yourselves. Each of
you should look not only to your own interests, but also to
the interests of others.*

Philippians 2:3-4

Most advertising seems to be aimed at convincing
people to "need" things they never needed before.
Billboards, web ads, commercials, and prod-
uct placements try to persuade us that we will be missing
something or will somehow be less of a person without their
product. After all, movie stars and athletes use the product. If
we follow suit, we can be like them. Salespeople use desire for
gain or fear of loss to motivate us to buy.

Frank Bettger started his career in sales as an underedu-
cated and unsuccessful man; but, as described in his book
How I Raised Myself From Failure to Success in Selling, he
discovered a secret that eventually made him one of the
most successful insurance salesmen of his day. Selling people
things they didn't need, Frank learned, was a frustrating and
unrewarding enterprise. Instead, he trained himself to make a
careful study of his clients' needs and then tried to help them
meet those needs. To do this, he had to listen to them and
truly be interested in their lives. That lesson proved to be the
beginning of a great American success story—and it's also one
of the keys to building healthy, lasting relationships.

JESUS OUR EXAMPLE

Frank Bettger gives us a good example of how powerful it is
to take interest in others, but we have an even more vivid
illustration in Jesus. He left His place in heaven and came to
earth to put our eternal
interests above His own.
"Each of you," Paul told
us earlier, "should look
not only to your own
interests, but also

**Jesus put aside what
would have been in His
own best interest for the
benefit of others.**

to the interests of others"—because this was the attitude that governed the way Christ lived among us. To
better understand His heart for us, we need to continue
reading in Philippians: "...who, being in very nature God, did not
consider equality with God something to be grasped, but
made himself nothing, taking the very nature of a servant, being made in human likeness. And being found in

appearance as a man, he humbled himself and became obedient to death—even death on a cross!" (Philippians 2:6-8)

Jesus put aside what would have been in His own best interest—including self-preservation—all for the benefit of others. Over the last two thousand years, He has won the hearts of millions upon millions of people. Beyond that, His Father "exalted Him to the highest place and gave Him the name that is above every name" (Philippians 2:9). Who is more famous in the earth than Jesus Christ? Even those who reject Christianity often admire His lifestyle and teaching. And to think, His "career" lasted only three years and ended in a criminal execution! It is amazing how this principle works in winning and keeping the hearts of others.

A POLITICIAN'S INTEREST IN OTHERS

J.L. Dawkins was the mayor of our city for seven straight terms. J.L. loved politics, because he loved people. Everyone felt they were J.L.'s good buddy; it seemed to be his gift. He was interested in what interested other people and in what they had to say. From sanitation workers to bankers and successful entrepreneurs, they all knew they had his ear—and it showed on Election Day. No one ever came close to unseating him. People didn't just vote for the Mayor; they voted for a friend. J.L., in the eyes of the city, was the picture of a true public servant.

Every politician would love such a relationship with his constituents. How did J.L. do it? He simply served others by being interested in what interested them. He could be found everywhere—talking to people, listening, laughing, and patting them on the back for their achievements. Day in and day out he showed individuals that what concerned them concerned him; what made them laugh made him laugh; what seemed important to them became important to him. When cancer started taking its toll on his body, the city's response demonstrated the level of entrance he had won into their hearts. Buildings and plazas were named for him. In the end, he was affectionately named "Mayor for Life."

THE EFFECT OF INTEREST AND CONCERN

All of us are naturally attracted to what interests us. So when we take an interest in what is important to others, we are showing interest in more than the thing itself. We are actually demonstrating interest in the person. When we afford them the opportunity to share their thoughts and hopes freely, we draw out the things that are close to their hearts, and so, little by little, we draw out their hearts themselves. Don't underestimate what a gift that can be to someone. Many people live in homes, work in offices, and study in schools where they have little or no freedom to discuss the things they cherish or delight in. When they find someone who shares that interest, an immediate bond is often the result.

But what if your wife is excited about needlework? Or what if your husband is into hunting and you can't stand the thought of killing Bambi? What if your teenager is into soccer instead of real football? How can a person be interested in something that is of no interest to them? Faking it isn't going to work; you can't see your 6'4" frame wedged in a chair for hours, fighting with teensy needles. And while camouflage has made some headway in the fashion world lately, you can't quite see your wife touching up her lipstick in a tree stand.

Think back to the beginning of one of your friendships. How did it begin? You met at work and the two of you clicked—same football team, same love of Mexican food, same terrible handicap in golf. But of course you don't share all the same interests. You never even thought about owning a boat (seemed like a lot of trouble to you). But your buddy had a boat, and one day at the grocery store you found yourself standing in the magazine section looking at boats while your wife was tracking down size three diapers. At the checkout, to your wife's amusement, you bought a magazine that featured your friend's boat. You don't really care all that much about boats, but Bob is a friend, and you do care about him. And he will care about you in return, because you have validated his passion for boating.

You hate contemporary art, but you spent hours walking through museum galleries when you dated that art major in college, didn't you? She could chatter for hours about this artist and that style, and you displayed your interest in her by giving attention to what was close to her heart. By doing this you showed her that she had a place in *your* heart, and as a consequence, you won a place in hers.

You don't have to buy a boat, learn to cross-stitch, take up painting, or master bow hunting. When your wife needs material for a new sewing project, go with her to the fabric store. When you get there, watch out for the guy sitting in the chair near the door, rolling his eyes and checking his phone. That guy is sending a message to his wife that you don't want to send to yours. In a thousand different ways, he's screaming *I don't care about this!* He doesn't realize that what she hears is: *in this area, you don't care about me.* She may be secure in other areas of their relationship, but when it comes to this passion of hers, she'll never risk opening up to him. She'll find other people and give that piece of her heart to them. But that guy is not you—oh no!

> We don't have to develop brand new passions to match the passions of those we love.

You are right there, leaning over your wife's shoulder, admiring her for the patience you obviously do not have, praising her for her generous gift of time to make this for her sister's new baby. She turns, holds up two bolts of cloth, and asks, "What do you think?" She isn't asking the lady who works there. She isn't asking the other woman looking through the solids. She is asking you—her friend, her husband, someone who values her by valuing what is important to her. What makes it even more special is that she knows that you really don't have any personal attraction toward sewing. She can only assume that you are there and involved because of the place she occupies in your heart.

As you leave the store, take another look at the guy slouching by the door. Aren't you glad you aren't him? Your wife is glad. She's thrilled with the man she has, and she's impressed that he's secure enough in his masculinity to go through fabrics and discuss patterns with her. As you climb into the car, you evaluate what that "gift" cost you—nothing. But what is the reward? A continued piece of your wife's heart—priceless!

People change and so do their interests. Again, we don't have to develop brand new passions to match the passions of those we love. But, like Frank Bettger, we do need to make a careful study of their continually changing needs and desires. Sit down with your spouse and ask questions. Talk to your kids—what makes them tick? Don't be satisfied with their initial answers. It may take a bit of time, but eventually, they will realize you really are interested in them, not just in keeping track of what tickles their fancy this month. Ask your clients where they hope to be in five years and how they plan to get there, even if it has nothing to do with buying your product.

When my daughter Annie was six, she discovered puzzles—not the hard wooden ones but the real ones, made of cardboard. With great excitement, she showed me the scant progress she had made the night before. Laura and I were headed out the door for our morning run, but I had a few minutes while my wife moved the laundry into the dryer and rehearsed instructions with the older children. I got down on the floor and showed Annie the number one rule in puzzle assembly—find the corners first. Then I instructed her on the number two rule—sort out the straight-edged pieces from the rest. She was thrilled. A whole new world of puzzle-making opened up to her; the days of piddly 100-piece puzzles were numbered in her book. I hate puzzles. Even as a kid, I always considered them a waste of time. But I love Annie, and at least for that week, Annie loved puzzles. So there I sat on the floor, finding corners and straight edges, until I was admonished by the "outside voice" coming from the little six-year-old mouth—"Dad, don't do the whole thing!" When I returned home from the run, I was the first to be greeted with the news of her progress. She thought I was the man! I took a few minutes to do something I don't enjoy. The reward? A continued piece of a little girl's heart.

No one has to live a friendless existence. Wherever there are people, there are passions that occupy their attention and time. All we have to do is find people and start asking them questions. Once we strike upon the topic of their passion, their mouth will generally open—followed closely by their heart. When you explore those areas of their lives with them, you serve people by putting their interests above your own. If it is a new relationship, you are putting yourself in a position to win their heart. If it is an existing relationship, you are building on what you already have.

> As we value others by taking an interest in what is important to them, we will touch their hearts.

Why let coworkers and friends care more about our loved ones than we do? Why let the woman who works across the hall have a route into the heart of your husband, just because you decided that showing interest in him was too time-consuming? Why let our children's peers steal their hearts, because our lives are too busy to find puzzle corners?

As we value others by taking an interest in what is important to them, we will touch their hearts. Those who apply this key and consistently put others' interests before their own will be some of the richest people relationally. Put this into practice in your own life and you will never be in want for friends or family.

CHAPTER FIVE

AVAILABILITY
MAKING ROOM FOR OTHERS IN CRISIS

*A new command I give you: Love one another. As I have
loved you, so you must love one another.*

John 13:34

*Carry each other's burdens, and in this way you will fulfill
the law of Christ.*

Galatians 6:2

There is no doubt that everyone in this life will experience
pain. All of us have had and will continue to have some
type of pain occur in our lives. I wish it weren't true.
Being in pain is bad enough, but being in pain alone
is almost unbearable. During Bible college, I was
experiencing a revisitation of what seemed to be all I had
eaten for the last year at one end and Montezuma's revenge

at the other in the wee hours of the morning. All alone in the dorm, cleaning up my own mess, I resolved that although these other guys might be great guys, being sick among them was a real drag. The next morning I called my mother, who was all too glad to take me in and nurse me to health.

Upon arriving at home, my body continued to test the limits of viral assault, but I can't tell you how much better I felt inside. Nestled in my old bed, I was comforted that she was in this thing with me to the end. Two days later I was back at the grind, more firmly convinced than ever that no one could take Mom's place. I would always be her boy (a fact I somewhat regretted when, at 30, she was still telling me it was too cold to go out without a hat), and she would always be Mom.

A NEW COMMANDMENT

Some people have wondered what Jesus meant when He told His followers that He was giving them a new commandment. Wasn't it the same as the old commandment? Jesus Himself had said that the greatest commandment was to "'Love the Lord your God with all your heart and with all your soul and with all your mind.' And the second is like it: 'Love your neighbor as yourself.'" (Matthew 22:37, 39) But in our passage from John, He says He is giving them a new commandment. What's new about it? Notice that the commandment drawn from the Old Testament tells us to love our neighbor as *ourselves*. The new commandment, however, raises the bar; now He is telling them to love others as *He* has loved them.

How is it that we have been loved by God? Paul told the Roman believers that "God demonstrates His own love for us in this: While we were still sinners, Christ died for us." (Romans 5:8) When we were in the greatest crisis of all, unable to help ourselves, Jesus Christ laid down His life for us. He loved us by reaching us in the midst of our most desperate need, even though we had no appetite for Him or His ways. Before we could search, before we knew to search, He was there. It was a sacrificial love—the kind that makes itself available to people in need, the kind that sees it through to the end. From now on, Jesus tells us, we are to love others like that.

THE PRINCIPLE OF AVAILABILITY

I call this the principle of availability. Many people claim to be available to their loved ones. I've heard people say, "He knows I am available to him. He can call on me whenever he wants." But I'm talking about something much deeper than that. I'm talking about making people a priority; about stepping up beside them when the chips are down. This is about seeing them through their crisis.

Joby Adams was a perfect example of an available life. I can't tell you the number of times when we were together that he had to stop to see how someone was doing. He knew everything about people's situations. He knew that Mr. John Doe's neighbor Mrs. Jane Smith had lost her house, that her oldest son had died of cancer a couple of years ago, and that she had been alone ever since. Joby ran into Mr. John Doe at the mall one day and learned that Mrs. Jane Smith had asked about him, so on the way back into town, we had to stop for just a minute. Mrs. Jones was also there, so we better go inside and see how everyone is doing. "How are you? And your son? Did he finish at State? Is he working nearby? When was the accident?" Before we were done he was saying, "Bless your heart, bless your heart," and fighting back tears. He was always there, always concerned, always a friend, and people loved him for it. They stood in line forever at his funeral, each thinking of themselves as a special friend of Joby. He had been their friend when they needed him; he had loved them as he had been loved by God. Joby made people a priority, and in return they let him into their hearts and lives.

A CRISIS TAKES TIME

When people go through tough times together, they establish a deep and lasting bond. The crucible of crisis forces people to depend on others at a level they would normally be uncomfortable with. Tears once shed in secret now flow for the privileged few to see. Hearts desperate for wisdom ask for advice they never sought before. The people who are holding your hand when the runaway comes through the door, or bringing you coffee at the late night vigil beside the sickbed, are the ones you often share the longest and deepest connection with. The friends who show up to rake the yard and mend the fence after your back surgery will spring fondly to your mind through the years.

> When people go through tough times together, they establish a lasting bond.

RECOGNIZING THE CRISIS

Oftentimes, though, our biggest challenge isn't pulling away from personal concerns to give proper attention to those in crisis—it's recognizing a crisis when it has arisen. The examples I gave earlier—a death in the family, a medical emergency—are obvious cases, but most crises are not so easy to spot. Missing these quieter crises is where the greatest damage is done.

Our trouble lies in the fact that we like to be the ones who define what constitutes a true crisis. We look at the circumstances and evaluate them by our own set of strengths and weaknesses, or our personal station in life. If we conclude that the person is at fault for bringing this upon himself or herself, we may be slower to reach out with compassion; sometimes we might not offer help at all. In reality, a crisis is defined as such by the person who is in it. Often what constitutes a crisis is not the thing itself, but how one feels about it at the time. To them, at that moment, it is a crisis, however firmly you may believe that it's not.

For example: say your nine-year-old daughter just found out that her best friend lied about her to the other students in her class. She is devastated. This was her best friend! Oblivious to the fact that you are deeply engrossed in trying to pay the bills with a checkbook that just won't balance, she comes running up to you, going on and on about something to do with friends and school, crying and talking, crying and talking. "Honey, go wash your face. You'll feel better then. I can't deal with this right now." After washing her face and not feeling any better, she calls another friend, who is glad to hear her out and walk her through it. After dinner, she asks if she can spend the night with her confidant. Off she goes with your permission; you knew she'd feel better if she washed her face. You have no idea that you gave away an opportunity to be her knight in shining armor and sent her off to cry on the shoulder of the little girl down the street.

Winning and keeping the hearts of others requires that we make ourselves available to those we love. When we do this, we communicate the place of priority they hold in our lives. Once they realize they have that place, they will protect the relationship with everything they have. You will defend a friend who has been in the trenches with you from the attack of hostile coworkers, even though it means taking some heat yourself. You don't mind going to the mat for those who stood up for you in your time of trouble.

This fact holds true even when the relationship is a harmful one. When Julie was cut from the cheerleading squad, Dad figured it was because she didn't really give it her all. "She's always had a problem with that," he reasons. "Besides, she needs to concentrate more on academics anyway." It's a shame Dad didn't read the previous chapter. If he had made her interests a priority, he might have known that Julie has dreamed of becoming a cheerleader for years. All her disappointment would have come pouring out, and he would have been able to share a piece of his life story with her. It

> What constitutes a crisis is not the thing itself, but how one feels about it at the time.

was football, not cheerleading, but it hurt the same way when his friends made the team but he was cut. He could have shared with her the comfort that eventually came to him, but he passed up the opportunity because he decided it wasn't a real crisis.

Now, instead of being in the safe arms of her father, she is in the arms of a boy from school who feels that she should have made the team. She has the talent. She has the looks. He's been watching her. Later, when Dad finally realizes that this relationship has become physical and destructive, Julie fights him tooth and nail. She loves this boy. He understands her. It's too bad Dad didn't discern the crisis that was before him when he had the chance. It's too bad he opted to define the crisis himself, instead of letting Julie define it and responding accordingly to her. Julie's bad choices are her own responsibility, but Dad left her vulnerable when she needed him most—and that was his responsibility.

I wonder how many men and women have wandered off into extramarital affairs simply because when they needed someone to talk to, their spouse was nowhere to be found and someone else stepped into the crisis? I wonder how many people have allowed good friendships to erode because they weren't there in their friend's time of need? In each of these cases and others like them, someone will come alongside and stand in the gap. They will be in a position to capture that heart.

A word of balance—I am not contending for being jerked around by attention-seekers who leap from one fabricated crisis to another. Sadly, some people use their problems as a method of attracting attention to themselves. They are not really interested in solving their problems; if the problems were ever solved, they would lose their attention-getting mechanism. Unfortunately, these poor souls will become known for the actors they are, and they will suffer without support in times of true need as a consequence of continually crying wolf.

We live in a world where everything fights for our time. If we are to truly value others, we must make the decision in advance to make them a priority. We do that by dropping lesser things for more important things, and by being there for them in the midst of their crisis, as they define crisis. Whoever does this is in a position to greatly impact the hearts of those around them.

C H A P T E R   S I X

RESPECT

ESTABLISHING A PERSON'S WORTH

Give everyone what you owe him…if respect, then respect; if honor, then honor.

Romans 13:7

I have a good friend who travels the world as a much sought-after speaker and a leader in a large and growing network of churches. His charisma has to be seen to be believed. Once while traveling to a speaking engagement of my own, I was hosted by some of the same people who had hosted him just months before. I heard them laughing over and over again about how he had called ahead and put his order in for a certain homemade cookie or favorite dessert. And they loved it! I knew I could never pull that off. Over the years, I often marveled at his magnetism and wondered how it worked; I was sure it had to be more than just his personality.

It first became clear when I heard him talking about some mutual friends of ours. I had considered them ordinary people, with no outstanding qualities; but not this fellow. Through his eyes, I saw them in a different light. He thought they were really something; small things I had overlooked stood out to him, and in response he honored and respected them. I heard it in his voice, and I knew that they must have heard the same thing.

Reflecting on our friendship, I saw that he had done the same with me on numerous occasions. A wonderful speaker himself, he needs no help from anyone, least of all me. But time and again over the years, he's called me to ask about some obscure statistic he couldn't put his hands on—and the conversation never stops there. He'll go on to ask my opinion about some current event or controversy; sometimes he'll invite me to comment on a situation in his own life, seeking fresh insight. I hate to be interrupted when I'm preparing for a sermon—it breaks my concentration and disrupts my flow— but I always tell my secretary to put his calls through. He respects my ideas, and in respecting my ideas, he respects me. He does that with everybody, and that is why people let him into their hearts so freely.

THE NECESSITY OF RESPECT

Too many of us think that respect is something we only owe to those who have climbed higher on the ladder of life than we have. To the layman, the medical student has a wealth of knowledge, but compared to a surgeon, the medical student has miles to go. Most of the people on the street would afford the medical student a fair measure of respect, simply because he was able to get into medical school. But they would not expect the surgeon to give the student a second thought. We give the boss respect. We have to—he's the boss. But we don't see a reason to show any special regard for our coworkers; after all, they're on the same rung that we're on.

We want honor and respect, but we are cautious and stingy in giving them out. It would be too much of a risk to honor the people below us on our social, educational, or economic ladder—suppose we give them delusions of grandeur? Worse yet, suppose we make ourselves look weak and insignificant by comparison? We might as well go ahead and say *Hey, Tim, feel free to consider yourself better than I am.* That would hardly be to our benefit—we too want to be noticed by others, to have people acknowledge and value us for who we are. The need for acceptance and approval is basic to human existence, a universal craving. Those who satisfy this hunger are the ones who will change lives.

The secret to my friend's magnetism was simply that he felt free to give respect to people no matter their station on the ladder. First, he didn't make himself the measure. He wasn't concerned about who was ahead or who was behind. Second, he found something of value in almost everyone he met. People perceived that he saw them as they saw themselves. Not only did he acknowledge them, he pulled them up to a status of respect higher than they were usually afforded. They were valued. True respect is rarely offered to most people, so they are irresistibly drawn to those from whom it comes.

RESPECT TURNS
REBELLIOUS HEARTS

The academy teachers and administrators regretted their decision to extend the school into the upper grades. If it had been one or two stray rebels scattered among the crowd, that would have been one thing; but by the time I came along, they had developed a group dynamic. I was armed with a love for them and one single truth: treat the junior high kids like high school kids, and the high school kids like college students, and you'll see remarkable changes in their behavior and in their response to you. At first, they came to my meetings because they wanted to hang out together, or because their parents made them. But my wife and I put into practice what little we knew. Looking back, the meetings were terrible, and I can only be thankful nobody ever broke out a video camera. But the kids kept coming and hanging out in our apartment. When I drove my little green Volkswagen Bug through the parking lot, they would mob me, standing on the bumper or piling inside (did you knew that 10 teenagers can fit into the back seat of a VW Bug?) They loved us!

One day, I noticed through the window that an administrator was walking into one of the classrooms filled with my students. When he didn't come out for several minutes, I smelled trouble, so I went to see what they had gotten into now. The moment I arrived on the scene, it was clear that the battle lines had been drawn. Later a group of relieved students stood around me, thanking me for coming. "When you walked in," they said, "we felt like the cavalry had arrived!" What had we done to receive such a place in their hearts? We respected them, even though they were beneath us in station and age, and even though their behavior sometimes created trouble.

But—and this is key—we didn't respect them without merit. I made them my tutors on contemporary culture. I asked them to help me decide what we should do for fun. I joked with the guys about sports as if they were my equals; Laura sat on the couch watching movies with the girls. They became part of our family. We valued their opinions and sought their ideas about things. But most of all, we listened to them—really listened. Even when we disagreed, we didn't write them off as ignorant or rebellious teens. We interacted. In effect, rather than talking down to them, we pulled them up on the ladder, sat down on a common rung, and talked.

HOW DO WE TREAT THOSE AROUND US?

When the air conditioning repairman comes to your house, how do you treat him? Do you evaluate him by comparing his bank account to yours? Or do you treat him as an equal because he is a human? In fact it goes further than that—you should respect him for the expert he is. If you had known what to do with your air conditioner, you would never have called for his assistance. Acknowledge the place he has earned and treat him as your superior in this arena, granting him the respect he deserves.

Have you ever served in the Armed Forces? If not, then the nineteen-year-old PFC has achieved something you have not. Honor him for his commitment to his nation; respect him for the service he has rendered and the accomplishment of making it through Basic. When you go to a restaurant, do you plan to discuss your order with the cook yourself, or pick it up from the kitchen when it's ready? Then respect the waitress for the service she provides. She is doing what you would not do. Don't evaluate her by your station in life. Don't measure her socially, educationally, or economically. Value her because she is human, and respect her for the job she does.

This idea is powerful! Take another look at your children. They have expertise in some areas way beyond your personal skill level. When was the last time you found yourself in a high school gym class? Things are different now than when you were in school. Don't try to be the family high school expert. Your opinion on a given subject is valid, but so is the opinion of a child, friend, or spouse who sees a different point of view. Give them the same honor you want for yourself—the right to have an opinion. This doesn't mean that you abrogate your role as the parent. Your ideas on drugs and premarital sex should carry the day, but not every topic is that weighty. You might ask your nine-year-old, instead of his coach, what "off-sides" means during his soccer match. You might break out the map and discuss alternate routes with your teenager while on a family vacation.

My two older girls are great dancers, and my wife is a natural, but she hasn't had the training that they've had. I will find them in the kitchen or the hallway, arms outstretched in some position called by some French name, passing on some new step to their mother, all initiated by Mom. "Okay, show me again," and away they go. (They just run me out of the room and laugh when I give it a shot.) My wife is allowing the students to become the teachers; she is giving them respect and, on a deeper level, keeping the place she has in their hearts. Respect is a statement of a person's value, and people always stay close to those who regularly give them the honor they long for.

We are surrounded by people who have had experiences we have not had, and who have learned things we have not learned. If nothing else, they are experts on the topic of their own lives, and there is tremendous value in that. If a coworker has been on a trip to a part of the world you have not seen, let her be the expert. Don't quote everything you've ever read in Reader's Digest on the subject. In fact, take another step and ask questions—with interest. Make it personal. On several occasions, I have asked a waitress for her opinion about the discussion at our table. More than once I have been impressed with the response. But more importantly, I have given a gift.

Respect is a statement of a person's value.

Who said a spouse or a friend has to have the same training or experience as you to make valid input into your vocational situation? Chances are, whatever you do has something to do with people. Although you know your job, certainly you wouldn't claim to have cornered the market on people skills. More importantly, although your wife or father might not know everything pertaining to your job, they do know you. Another perspective on you might be helpful. People sometimes say to me, "I don't want to tell you how to do your job, but…"—to which I reply, "Please tell me how to do my job!" True, I've been a pastor for more than thirty years, but I can't begin to count the insights I have gleaned from someone on the outside looking in.

You can begin today to cultivate a new magnetism in your life. Look for qualities, skills, and knowledge in those you love that are worthy of respect. Seek out ways to honor people. Decide to acknowledge that every person you meet has something in his or her life that merits your admiration; everyone can teach you something. Determine now that you will reject the impulse to be the expert, and jettison the idea that you need to defend your rung on the ladder by withholding honor and respect from those around or beneath you. Hearts will open in new ways and at deeper levels as you apply this principle at home, at work, and at play.

TIME

THE KEY TO UNLOCKING A HEART

There is a time for everything, and a season for every activity under heaven...

Ecclesiastes 3:1

See then that you walk circumspectly, not as fools but as wise, redeeming the time, because the days are evil.

Ephesians 5:15-16

Young or old, rich or poor, male or female, we all have a few things in common. The clock, for one: each person on the face of the earth gets 60 seconds in every minute, 60 minutes in every hour, 24 hours in every day, and 365 days a year. We also share the same funny ideas about time. We talk about saving time, but no bank stores minutes to be used on a rainy day. We complain that we don't have time, even though we all have twenty-four hours in every day. The truth is, we really don't understand time, and so we easily mismanage our lives in relation to it. Make no mistake—time is a powerful thing.

Our relationships are the most important aspect of our lives; they govern our happiness and shape our future. But the quality of those all-important relationships will be determined by the way we manage our time. We may say we value our daughter and would even die for her, but she has her doubts when, although willing to pay for ballet lessons, we never make it to her recitals. We can claim that our children are our first priority and that all our hard work is for them, but if they are raised by daycare workers rather than us, we shouldn't be surprised when, as teenagers, their deepest loyalties reside outside the home. Words are powerful, but they are also cheap; it's easy to throw out trite platitudes if that's what we think someone wants to hear. Whatever comes out of our mouths, the real measure of what we value is how we use our twenty-four hours a day. Say what you like about the intentions of your heart, but how you spend your time draws the veil on what you really are.

TIME IS LIFE

Underscore this—your time is literally your life! As your minutes, hours, and days go, so goes your life. The allocation of your time reveals your priorities. When your hobbies get most of your spare time instead of your wife, it is clear to her (and others as well) that you value the hobbies more than her. As a matter of fact, since it's your personal pleasure that draws you to the hobby, it isn't really the hobby that takes priority over your spouse—it's yourself. The only way for people to be a priority in your life is for them to have a portion of your time. You only have so much time, so when you spend a few of your precious hours with a person, you are making a statement of their value. You establish them as important. As the old saying goes, actions speak louder than words. How you spend your time is the yardstick of what you truly treasure.

The way you spend your time reveals what is in your heart, but it also has the power to affect what is in your heart. Since your time is your life, and since the way you spend it is directly connected to what is in your heart, whomever you spend time with is in a position to influence your heart.

THE NEGATIVE EFFECT OF TIME ON A RELATIONSHIP

This principle doesn't necessarily work to our advantage. Because our hearts go where our time goes, we put ourselves in a dangerous place by spending time alone with people of the opposite sex to whom we are not married.

Most of the time it starts innocently—a boss and his secretary burning the midnight oil to get that project in on time. The first night they order out for Chinese food. The next night they heat up something she threw together at home, anticipating another late night. He is grateful for her diligent service, and she admires his strong leadership. Over dinner each night they converse about the strengths and weaknesses of their respective marriages. No one's marriage is perfect. Soon her heart goes out to him and his to her. He hugs her goodnight; she hugs him back. On their way out the door, they linger—then he kisses her. And that begins it. What started as an innocent project at work winds up in an extramarital affair that destroys two families. All involved had underestimated the power of spending time alone with another. While it wouldn't be true to say that time spent alone with a member of the opposite sex will always result in a sexual relationship, this scene has been played out far too many times to ignore the power of this principle.

Sometimes the process stops at the "emotional affair." Sex never enters the picture in an emotional affair. It ends with his heart going out to her and/or her heart going out to him—nothing physical, just the excitement of getting emotional needs met by someone other than their spouses. This may seem harmless, since the physical line hasn't been crossed—but emotional affairs damage marriages as well. A marriage is built around the heart. When your heart goes out to a person, it belongs to that person. If that person is someone other than your spouse, then you are destroying your marriage from the inside out. The delight you give the other person, the attention you pay them, and the affection you show for them aren't rightfully theirs; they are being stolen from your spouse. Brick by brick you are dismantling the emotional fortress that was (or should be) your marriage, weakening it from within. Even if the emotional affair never becomes physical, the

When your heart goes out to a person, it belongs to that person.

consequences of giving your heart away may prove as fatal as taking a sledgehammer to the load-bearing walls of your house.

TIME ALONE WHILE DATING

Time alone with the opposite sex isn't a danger only married people should be wary of. Ted was in love with the girl of his dreams and I was trying to warn him about the dangers of time alone. "Don't trust yourself. Time alone puts you in a dangerous position. First your heart goes out, then your hormones, then your head, in that order. By the time your head catches up with your heart and your hormones, it will be too late." He didn't listen. In the end, he ruined what could have been a wonderful relationship.

As a society, we know better than to let sixteen-year-olds carry guns (too dangerous) or drink alcohol (too destructive). We limit when and where they can drive. We monitor who they hang out with and insist on a reasonable time to be home. But we will cheerfully send them out alone with the opposite sex for three hours, unsupervised. Their heart is already gone, their hormones constantly raging, and we sit at home peacefully reading the paper while they struggle— often in vain—to deny the natural urges within. They can't help it! They were made that way! But they were also given two parents to guide them through this time in their life.

According to the U.S. Department of Justice's National Sex Offender Public Website, about 1 in 5 teenage girls—that's 20%—report being subjected to physical and/or sexual abuse by their dating partner.[1] If you knew that your child had a 20% chance of being shot while walking through a certain neighborhood, you wouldn't even let them out of the house. That 20% only counts those who say "no" but are forced; the survey has no reference to those who, while on a date, say "yes!" Whatever contemporary culture may want us to believe, a young person can live a wonderful, healthy life without playing Russian roulette in the modern dating game. Laura's parents insisted that we "date" on the couch in their living room. We had a great time vacationing with each others' families, going to sports games, and getting together with friends. As a result, I grew close to her whole family, and we are still close. Laura's father, a retired Army lieutenant colonel, even served on my staff for several years.

THE POSITIVE EFFECT OF TIME TO BUILD UP RELATIONSHIPS

Spending time alone with someone unwisely is a treacherous trail—but spending time alone with them *wisely* is the ticket to building relationships that will last a lifetime.

Some years ago I was invited to speak at a convention in Uganda. One of the other speakers at the convention, a friend of mine, brought his two oldest children with him. After he finished his part of the convention, he and his kids were headed to Lake Victoria, where they planned to log

---

[1] "Raising Awareness About Sexual Abuse: Facts and Statistics." National Sex Offender Public Website, accessed April 12, 2016, https://www.nsopw.gov/en-US/Education/FactsStatistics?AspxAutoDetectCookieSupport=1#reference

some quality time together before his son and daughter went off to college. They were great kids, and before they left, I told him how much I enjoyed spending time with them. He quickly replied, "It's not hard to raise great kids!" How perfectly he illustrated my point! The reason he had such great kids was that he made them a priority in his life. In giving his time to them, he had given his heart and established their value. In return, they had given their hearts to him.

My wife and I found that as our children got older, family scheduling became a nightmare. Laura has had decades of experience teaching our children at home, and she does a great job—several of them went to college on academic scholarships—but it's always a difficult balancing act. On top of that, she's been called on more and more to speak in various settings, and my responsibilities have broadened and brought new pressure into our family too. The kids' activities multiply with every year.

Despite all these balls in the air, we knew how important it was to the health of our marriage to make a point of spending time alone with each other. Laura has been running each morning for years. It keeps her healthy and provides tremendous stress relief. Years ago, I began to run with her. Rain or shine, hot or cold, we spend one hour together on the road each day. On our day off, we culminate our run with breakfast. By no means are we setting any speed records—it is connection time. We talk the whole time (except for hills). This time alone has bonded us together, bolstered our communication, and enabled us to thrive in this period of our lives.

THE GREAT INVESTMENT

When you give your time to someone, you are investing your life. Invest well. Time spent in front of the television probably doesn't count as family time, but time wrestling on the floor with the boys does. What ever happened to meals together? Even if your family schedule makes it tough to get everyone around the same table at once, some things are worth fighting for.

I appreciate the attitude my older children have on this score. They like hanging out with friends like anyone else, but we have tried to model the value of time together for them by giving our time to them. Does investment in family pay dividends? One night my three oldest sons—at the time ages 16, 18, and 20—hatched an idea. They wanted to go to the movies with their mother and father. My two oldest daughters thought that was a great idea and offered to watch the younger ones. How many young men want to hang out with their parents? I call that a dividend!

But Michael, you might be thinking, *you don't realize how busy I am! Where am I going to find all the time I need to invest in my spouse, children, parents, siblings, friends, boss, coworkers, and clients?* Remember, we all have the same amount of time. It all depends on how we choose to use it. Most of what happens in our lives just happens; we don't plan it. Other times we commit to something without taking into account the cost in hours. Before we know it, our lives are pulled in so many directions we can't even keep up. Then we read a chapter like this one, and we feel even more out of control.

One place to start is with the time we spend on ourselves. I've known people—you probably know some too—who say they have no time for their family but can always find time for a round of golf. Others can never clear out enough space in their schedule to go on a date with their spouse, but they can always work overtime to earn a few extra bucks. We can't miss our favorite TV show; reading the morning paper is a sacred rite; and so on.

Sometimes we have to set aside the lesser things for the important things. With my schedule, my time is really tight; but I have determined to be a family man, not just in word but in deed. I used to be a pretty fair tennis player, but I haven't hit a ball in years. I traded it for our kids' soccer matches and breakfast with my wife. I get my exercise with Laura, and a majority of my friends don't play tennis anyway. Major on others and minor on self. The reward always outweighs the sacrifice!

YOUR TIME INVESTMENT PLAN

What steps can you take today to improve your management of time, so as to make the most of your investment in others? Stop right now and take stock. A few pointers might help:

1. Who is really important to you? Rank them. Is your boss more important to you than your spouse? Are your clients or coworkers more valuable to you than your children?

2. What is most important to our loved ones? If our goal is to communicate value to them, time put into those

activities will yield the highest returns. Attending a play with your theater-loving wife will produce greater results than watching the Twins beat the Red Sox.

3. How can we optimize the schedule we have to yield greater results? Say your husband takes your son to soccer matches on Saturdays—can you make it a family affair? When you put the children to bed, how about telling a short story from your childhood? When you are running errands, swing by a friend's house and invite them along.

4. What potentially dangerous traps, created by time alone with others, should we avoid? Are we in the habit of eating lunch alone with coworkers of the opposite sex? Is there a person at work towards whom we are attracted?

As with our personal finances, we need a time investment plan. Don't wait—develop one and put it in place as soon as you can. The more skillful we become in spending our twenty-four hours a day, the more relational dividends we will reap and the more we will win the hearts of those we love.

CHAPTER EIGHT

COMMUNICATION
THE LIFELINE TO EVERY RELATIONSHIP

Let no unwholesome word proceed from your mouth, but only such a word as is good for edification according to the need of the moment, that it may give grace to those who hear.

Ephesians 4:29 (NASB)

Cindy had taken all she was going to take; Harold had pushed her over the edge. She knew what she had to do—but he'd never let her simply walk out the door. So to throw him off course, Cindy bought tickets to a game a couple of weeks away and gave them to him at dinner. Three days later, still looking forward to the game, Harold came home to a house that was now only partially furnished. The pictures of their children were gone; so were her clothes. Cindy had moved it all into an apartment across town. She never came home.

I asked Cindy what had happened to make her so resolute in her decision. She told me that one morning before work, in the middle of a heated argument, she had mentioned their pending wedding anniversary. Harold's response floored her. She realized at once that whatever else he said, he didn't really love her. Their marriage was dead, and she felt like a fool for not seeing it sooner. What had Harold said? Just to score a few points in the argument, as he stepped out the door, he hurled these words at her: "What anniversary? We don't even have a marriage to celebrate!" Feeling triumphant, he closed the door behind him and drove the car away, never realizing he had driven her away too. Those crushing words proved to be the straw that broke the camel's back.

I bet you heard this tired old rhyme as much as I did growing up: "Sticks and stones can break my bones but words will never hurt me." How many children have quoted that line to a playground antagonist? But words carry more weight than any stick or stone. Words have galvanized the hearts of the masses and mobilized whole nations, to the end that they even send their sons to war. They **If we want to win and keep the hearts of others, we need to master the art of communication.** have enchanted souls and stolen hearts. Loved ones wait with bated breath outside the emergency room hoping for the words, "He made it," while fearing the words, "I'm sorry. We did all we could." Words can torment us, destroy us, inspire us, and empower us. Make no mistake—words are potent things.

A LIFELINE

In the middle of the 20th century, salvage diving was an even more dangerous profession than it is now. Divers, encased in cumbersome pressurized suits, dropped via cables into the sea, accelerating their descent with lead-weighted shoes. Once on the bottom, they were totally dependent upon one all-important tube running from the ship to their suit: their lifeline, carrying a mixture of gases necessary to sustain human life. Cut the line, and the diver dies.

Relationships are also sustained by a lifeline. Every relationship is totally dependent on communication to continue its existence. In fact, each of the six keys already mentioned relies on this foundation. Love, availability, faith, respect, and interest might as well not exist if you don't communicate them to the other person; and time is so important because it is your opportunity to do that. If we want to develop successful relationships by winning and keeping the hearts of others, we need to master the art of communication. Without it, our relationships will die as surely as the diver whose lifeline is cut.

THE QUALITY OF COMMUNICATION

Not all communication is helpful. In fact, as we saw with Harold and Cindy, some types of communication are harmful. Returning to the example of the deep-sea diver—it's not enough for him just to have that tube. Something has to be flowing through it for it to do him any good. If nothing is traveling through it, he might just as well have no lifeline at all. But assuming that something is passing through the diver's tube, the quality of the mixture must be monitored. One might suppose that pure oxygen is pushed into the suit of the diver, but pure oxygen would be as dangerous to him as no oxygen at all. Up on the surface, we don't breathe pure oxygen; we breathe the combination of gases found naturally in the atmosphere. We are very sensitive creatures. Too much carbon dioxide or too much oxygen and the diver could suffer irreparable damage. That same ideal mixture that we enjoy on the surface must be provided to the diver; the quality of what passes through the tube is vital to the life of the man below.

In a relationship, silence is lethal, just as the diver's lifeline does him no good unless something is flowing. But the *quality* of the communication in our relationships is as important to their wellbeing as the *presence* of communication. The quality of your connection to another person depends as totally on the quality of what you convey to them as the diver's survival does on his proper mixture of gases.

PUTRID COMMUNICATION

Paul the Apostle instructed the early Ephesian believers on this topic with the following admonition: "Let no unwholesome word proceed from your mouth, but only such a word as is good for edification according to the need of the moment, that it may give grace to those who hear." (Ephesians 4:29, NASB) The original Greek word that is translated as "unwholesome word" literally means "putrid." When my trash can outside gets dirty, we might say it smells bad, even terrible. But after sitting out in the hot North Carolina August sun for a week, filled with the remains of a poolside fish feast, the stench can peel the paint off the car! That's putrid.

Paul instructs us not to let anything of that nature come out of our mouths. Why? Because words have power, and the wrong kinds of words can kill or irreparably damage a relationship. As Solomon wrote, "Death and life are in the power of the tongue." (Proverbs 18:21, NKJV) With the tongue we can kill relationships by damaging people. How many times have we said something we immediately regretted? Even as the words leave our lips, regret takes root in our hearts and we wish we could reel them back in and rephrase, or swallow them altogether. But the look on their face tells us it's far too late; our words have already done their damage. In that moment, the notion that "words will never hurt me" is overshadowed by the reality that death is in the power of the tongue. Those who are on the receiving end of putrid communication would gladly take a rock or two in place of the pain that words can bring.

Damaging words don't just hurt the people they're aimed at; their consequences extend to a wider sphere. Paul identifies that sphere as "those who hear." When a principal rips into one of his teachers in front of the rest of the faculty, everyone in range of the tirade is defiled. Who knows what effect the scene will have on the people in earshot around the corner, or how the relationships of all the parties will be impacted? Those overhearing may lose respect for the principal, their coworker, or both. They may even avoid contact with the principal, fearful of becoming his next target. Or take a husband and wife battling it out in the living room at home—it isn't the parents who suffer most. It's the children who are standing by, listening to the ones they love the most tearing each other down. In many cases, the winner of the conflict becomes the loser in the sight of the sons and daughters, since the one more hurt draws out their sympathy.

Sometimes "those who hear" weren't even in earshot when painful words were spoken. Suppose the teacher who was chewed out repeats the whole tirade to the parent of one of his students, adding his own interpretive twist. That parent, it so happens, is on the same bowling team as the principal. Now the relationship between the principal and his friend is being undermined. Not only does the principal have no opportunity to present his side of the story, he probably has no idea the friend has heard about it. The next time their paths cross at the bowling alley, he's bewildered by the cold greeting he receives. He can't figure out why this person's opinion of him has suddenly changed. If he'd had any idea that his vicious words were going to boomerang in such a fashion, he might have exercised more restraint in the first place.

Most people find it easy to tear others down. It is human nature to be critical when dealing with others. Out of pride and insecurity, we instinctively measure others by the opinion we hold of ourselves. We ignore the strengths we see in them, especially those that highlight our personal weaknesses, and we major on the faults of others, especially those that fall into the areas in which we normally shine. The Bible identifies many kinds of communication that kill, including:

Angry Words	Lying (Exaggeration)
Hasty Words	Flattery
Rash Words	Gossip
Harsh Words	Slander
Condemning Words	Complaining
Unkind Words	Cursing
Bitter Words	Quarreling
Mocking Words	Scoffing
Foolish Words	Comparison
Critical Words	Backbiting

It is hard to read that list without finding something we have done wrong, perhaps even habitually. Remember, every need provides an opportunity for building up, even the needs we create with our own damaging words! With a little effort and an exercise of humility, we can learn the art of affirmation. Take a few steps back and evaluate yourself. Are you affirming in your relationships? Do people look forward to being with you, because they always leave your company feeling built up? It is just as easy to build others up as it is to tear them down, and it is many times more rewarding! Remember what Solomon said: "Death *and* life are in the power of the tongue." (Proverbs 18:21, NKJV)

WORDS CAN BRING LIFE

When Paul told the Ephesian believers to let no putrid words escape them, he also told them what words they should be saying: the kinds of things that edify (or build up) others. Such words, Paul says, impart grace to all who hear. To mention just a few:

Words That Give Honor
Encouraging Words
Words That Bring Hope
Words That Promote Faith
Consolation
Instruction
Rebukes (See Prov. 9:8)
Edification/Words That Build Up
Guidance
Counsel
Words That Bring Joy/Laughter

The list of ways in which words can build up is endless. Paul used the phrase "according to the need of the moment". Wherever there is a need, there is an opportunity to build others up through our interaction with them. We must learn to use the needs of those around us as signposts, pointing to occasions for edification. When a coworker is under obvious stress about a project, encourage him by reminding him of past successes. When your spouse is frustrated by the pressures of having too much month at the end of the money, a positive word can go a long way. Telling a struggling employee that you admire the quality of his or her work is a great way to break them out of a creative slump. Remember, too, that sometimes effective communication requires no words at all. Sitting beside a friend in a hospital waiting room, holding her hand, and keeping her coffee cup filled communicates more support than a thousand words could ever convey.

When we build up the people around us with our words and actions, those to whom we speak are not the only winners. Remember the sphere defined as "those who hear" from Ephesians 4:29? The indirect recipients of edification are built up as well. Think of the times you have read an inspiring story or heard a great testimony. All those down the line are built up as your spouse repeats the wonderful thing you said to them. Employees eagerly spread the compliment paid to them by the boss. Children prosper in an environment where parents routinely value each other with their words.

As much as damaging words, affirming words have a marvelous boomerang effect. What do employees think of a boss who admires their work and tells them so? What do children think of a father who makes it clear that he loves their mother? When sons and daughters recognize their parents as their greatest cheerleaders, increased loyalty is the parents' prize. Your words have the power to build, and everyone loves to be built up. Edifying words actually give grace to those who hear them, thus producing life. That which tears down naturally repels people, but they are irresistibly drawn to that which gives life. Mastering the art of affirmation is the greatest gift you could give yourself. When you affirm others, you cannot escape the impact on your own reputation. Simply put, you become attractive to people.

Communication is the lifeline of every relationship, but the quality of what passes through that lifeline determines the health of those relationships. Just as bad air can slowly kill a deep-sea diver, negative and hurtful words destroy people. And just as the right gases, carefully mixed and monitored, can enable the diver to work beneath the surface for hours, so healthy communication can keep a flow of life in our interaction with others, producing strong and lasting relationships.

The first step towards health is knowing what needs to be healed. Take one more look at the list of harmful ways we can communicate to others. Have you used any of those in some of your relationships? As hard as it may seem, purpose now to go to each of those people and seek their forgiveness. Humble yourself and take responsibility for the pain you have caused them. Be very careful what you promise. When we are just beginning to build a new habit, failure is certain, especially in matters pertaining to the tongue. Telling your spouse that you will never criticize them again is probably making a promise you cannot keep. A more realistic approach might be simply to tell them that you are working on this area of your life.

Successful relationships are built by winning and keeping the hearts of others. Hearts are won and kept as we apply the principles of love, faith, interest, availability, respect, and time. But these principles are only as effective as our channels of communication. Never forget—"bad air" kills, but affirmation produces life!

CHAPTER NINE

NEITHER MAGIC NOR MANIPULATION

We live today in what I call a "microwave society." Everywhere you go, people want it now and they want it hot. But true lasting relationships don't work like Easy Mac or ramen. They work like crock pots—they take effort and lots of time. When a relationship turns south, people often come to me for counsel. Some take the advice they receive and begin to work their way out of the hole they have dug for themselves, putting in the effort of applying the principles we've talked about as they try to win back the heart they see slipping away—but others leave disheartened. They had waited much too long, and they were looking for a quick fix—a magic wand that could wave their problem away. Let me make it clear: these ideas are not magic formulas.

THE MYTH OF THE MAGICAL SHORTCUT

Magic is big today, driven by a society that demands instant answers to problems caused by more complicated factors. Magic, by definition, is an attempt to override the will of others by applying unseen powers that will force people to do things, feel things, or become things against their will. If you're looking for that kind of control over someone else's heart, this book will disappoint you. These principles contain no magical power of enchantment to make people love you. They only create the environment where hearts can be won and facilitate the process by which they can be kept.

While it is true that no one is safe from the potential theft of their heart, it is also true that no one's heart is really stolen against their will. Hearts are won step-by-step or piece-by-piece. As we serve someone or spend time with them, their heart opens to us a little more. Even if at first we weren't on their list of favorite people, by encouraging them or listening to their life story, we are putting ourselves in a position to work our way into their hearts. Day by day, the recipient of our effort has the opportunity to change their mind about us, and more importantly, change the status of their heart toward us. But they can choose not to.

Hearts are won step-by-step or piece-by-piece.

Faith, availability, interest, and the other ideas we've talked about are not ingredients in a potion that we can sneak into our coworker's lunch to make them fall in love with us. We are dealing with people, not objects. In the end, our coworker will have to participate in the process and make choices along the way. When they feel their heart going out, they must choose to let the process continue along its natural course unhindered, or decide to cut off the relationship where it stands, halting any further progress. Perhaps they are married and begin to recognize that all this time spent with a coworker is detrimental to their relationship with their spouse. Thank God these truths are not part of a magic formula that can override our will or force us into something we do not want.

No relationship is free from risk. Even if you apply all seven keys perfectly, there's no guarantee you won't experience pain at some point from someone who refuses to respond to you as you'd hoped they would. What I can guarantee is that these applications will put you in the best position to win and keep the hearts of others.

MANIPULATION

Even though the keys we've talked about are not magical spells, that doesn't mean that people can't try to apply their power in the wrong ways. Unscrupulous people bent on self-satisfaction can twist any truth to their own ends, and self-centered people will use whatever means necessary to get what they want. But truth applied out of false motives is incapable of producing lasting results. Manipulation always destroys.

Webster's Dictionary defines manipulation as "to control or play upon by artful, unfair, or insidious means especially to one's own advantage."[1] Manipulation has self at the center, and it sees people as pawns who provide the benefits of life for personal consumption. It is a perversion of everything I have tried to put forward in this book. Over the years I have seen manipulation take various forms.

PUSHING OTHERS AWAY

Fred was convinced that Andrea was the one for him, so he pursued her with a vengeance. If he were to read this book today, he might assume that he had done everything right, but he never got the reward he had hoped for. Andrea ran from him with everything she had, and Fred ended up chasing her right into the arms of another man, whom she fell in love with and eventually married.

Fred had two problems that stripped the power right out of the truths he applied, actually causing them to have a reverse effect. First, his motive was self-centered. His care for Andrea was not truly driven out of a desire for what best benefited her; he wanted a wife for himself. In the end, Fred's actions were all about what was good for Fred. Second, he pushed. Think about that word *push* for a second. You can never push anything toward yourself; pushing is an outward motion that moves things away from you. A pushy attitude betrays a heart dominated by its own agenda. The moment someone begins to push, they try to force that agenda on the other person's

---

[1]Merriam-Webster, s.v. "manipulation." Accessed April 12, 2016, http://www.merriam-webster.com/dictionary/manipulation.

will, and that repulses people. Make it clear in your mind that when you push, you push people away.

When a father decides that after years of totally neglecting his teenager, they are now going to be best buddies and weekly golfing partners, he runs the risk of driving his son away. When a young man sets his sights on a woman and follows her everywhere she goes, she ends up feeling stalked, not admired. If you attempt to spend every waking moment with your new friend in the dorm room across the hall, it won't be long before she's avoiding you altogether.

GROVELING

Sometimes a manipulator heads in the opposite direction. Rather than pushing, they take the "poor me" approach. Mistaking sympathy for love, they cast themselves in the role of the victim, hoping the emotion they draw out of people will somehow mutate into something upon which they can build.

In the last chapter, we heard how Harold had driven away his wife with his cruel words. If that had been all that happened, perhaps Cindy could have been persuaded to return. But against all advice, Harold first pursued Cindy by pushing his way back into her life: "You can't do this. We have been married twenty years, and I won't stand for it!" He quickly learned that this was a dead end road, but then he tried another approach with increasingly disastrous results—he groveled. He quit eating well and made sure she noticed. He sent flowers, something he hadn't done in years, with notes begging her to come home. He visited her at work, and with pleading eyes, spoke of the love he held for her in his heart. This form of manipulation rarely works for three reasons.

First, to grovel you must completely set aside all measure of self-respect. When we are in this mode we rarely realize what a pathetic spectacle we make of ourselves—trudging around hangdog, whining, and so on. But others certainly see what a scene we're making, and people have no respect for those who do not respect themselves. Groveling only makes us appear pitiful, and the only emotion that elicits is pity—a far cry from the love we crave.

Second, groveling is another form of pushing! It seeks to fulfill its own desire by forcing the departed heart to come back. The method differs, but the motive is the same. Self is at the center, and it does whatever it can think of to make the loved one comply with its agenda.

Third, one of the foundational truths we keep coming back to is that hearts are kept the same way they are won. Do you suppose Harold begged Cindy, with desperation in his voice, the first time he asked her out?

The most valuable things in life take time to cultivate.

Did he grovel outside her apartment, or interrupt her every day at work to get her to notice him? No way! He instinctively applied several (or all) of the keys we've learned about, and he won her heart. When her heart strayed away, he should have revisited the methods he used at first, with even greater patience, giving her all the space she needed to allow for the rekindling of affection.

CHANGING ROLES

Another form of manipulation manifests itself when people step outside the normal parameters of their position to pursue a relationship. At first glance this might appear noble, but a deeper look reveals a selfish heart at work.

A friendless college professor decides to step out from behind his podium to try hanging out with the guys. Off-balance and intimidated by his authority, the students reluctantly invite him out for a night on the town. By the evening's end, they have lost all respect for the professor and see him as weak and pitiful. Mothers and fathers, reaching for the heart of a child they see slipping away, sometimes bail on their role as parent and take on the role of friend. But learning the lingo and donning the duds won't erase twenty-plus years of age separation and cultural orientation. Lowering yourself from parent to the position of friend will not win the respect of your child. In fact, it's very likely to have the opposite effect. What will your son say when his friends ask, "Bro, what's up with your dad? What kind of trip is he on?" Now you add embarrassment to the list of indictments your son has against you.

Why is this manipulation? Because it seeks to maneuver people into a closer relationship, without facing the tough questions about why the current relationship has become distant. Once again, self is at the center. All of the seven keys we've studied place the other person at the center. Our focus is on loving them, having faith for them, serving them, being available to them—because we enjoy them, not because we want them to enjoy us. If our focus is on getting back what we once had for our own benefit, we betray ourselves and reveal our true heart. In the end, we make matters worse, not better.

Our approach should be to first humble ourselves and take a look at where we have allowed for the downward spiral of the relationship. Which of the seven keys have we habitually neglected? In some cases, we might find out that we have been faithful for the most part, and that the other person is the one who has strayed. Perhaps someone else has stolen their heart. Nevertheless, let's begin with ourselves, attempting to detect what adjustment we might need to make.

Second, take inventory of the needs of your loved one. Create a plan to apply the seven keys to meet those needs. Make your loved one the focus. They are the one you are seeking to benefit; let any benefit that comes to you be a bonus. Your main reward is in seeking their highest good.

Third, be patient! Don't be too quick to assess the results of what you are doing. Things sometimes get worse before they get better. If a spouse, for instance, has allowed their heart to go out to a coworker, your overtures of affection may increase the guilt they feel. Normally, the first stage of that conviction demonstrates itself with increased irritation or a determination to avoid you for prompting those guilty feelings. Be patient and get creative. What you are doing is having the desired effect.

Trying to override someone else's will to get what you want is always wrong. There are no shortcuts in building strong relationships. The most valuable things in life take time to cultivate. Manipulation—whether we push, grovel, or step out of our place—will always produce negative results, because manipulation only cares about *me*. A successful relationship isn't about you; it's always about the other person.

OF DOGWOODS
& DOGFIGHTS

No one ever cuts down a dogwood tree, and yet there I was, cutting down the second one in as many months. And this one was right in the middle of my front yard! I felt like a botanical failure, especially by comparison with my family. My father doesn't just have a green thumb, he has a whole green forearm; he can get stuff to grow in concrete. And my mother knows the name of every plant in the book! As I cut the once-beautiful tree into pieces for curbside pickup, I eyed the most spectacular of the remaining dogwoods in my yard. The branch in the middle had dropped all its leaves and was slowly drying up. I was losing another one! Something had to be done.

I called in an expert who immediately diagnosed the problem. These trees weren't struck by lightning, and they hadn't been hit by a car. They were being eaten by a disease. I was off the hook, right? *I am not responsible for this. Some tree disease got them—just bad luck.* Wrong! My expert squatted down by the trunks of the remaining trees and showed me the problem. As it turned out, in my zeal to manicure my front lawn as perfectly as possible, every time I cut the grass I had cut too closely to the trees. The constant nicking over the four years we had lived in the house had damaged the protective bark around the base of each tree, allowing access to destructive diseases. Without realizing it, I had been killing my trees with my own hands. The trees ultimately died due to the effects of long-term damage.

RELATIONAL NEGLECT

When a relationship dies, it usually withers just like my dogwoods did. Someone has neglected to do regular maintenance on it and allowed the relationship to slowly deteriorate.

On our family farm in Michigan stands an old walnut tree that has been struck more than once by lightning. You might think a storm as severe as that would destroy the tree, but it has survived. Most storms that spring up overnight, even the nasty ones, can be weathered; in fact, going through a storm or two actually makes plants stronger. Before we lost our dogwoods, they had lived through two devastating hurricanes, and fared well. It wasn't the short-term crisis that did the trees in—and usually, it isn't the short-term crisis that does a relationship in, either. As we saw in the chapter on availability, crises tend to pull us together. In the middle of the storm we may despair of ever making it, but when the clouds dissipate we find ourselves in the sun again, working side by side to make things better. Families in times of financial struggle may fear the pressure will tear them apart and destroy their children, but in the end that pressure often serves to drive them closer together.

Of course, sometimes the lightning strike does kill the tree on the spot. If a husband, after years of hidden affairs, is suddenly discovered, the blow may completely wipe out that marriage. But even in these cases, it's often more than the single strike of lightning that destroyed the relationship. Long-term damage probably encroached over the years, allowing disease to creep inside and weaken the relationship. When the storm clouds came and the lightning struck, the relationship lacked the strength to stand.

The point is simple—relationships are not usually lost due to short-term crisis. They erode over time. Every week, I contributed to the demise of my dogwoods, never realizing what I was doing. These seven keys we've been talking about are not optional in building lasting relationships. They are what cause relationships to develop in the first

Relationships are not usually lost due to short-term crisis, but erode over time.

place, and what enable them to last. If we do not take the trouble to apply them, we can expect to find ourselves on the curb someday, piling up the remnants of our relationships.

SOWING SEEDS AND NURTURING

There is good news on the flip side of this coin. The trees that enjoy long-term maintenance are the ones that live the longest and produce the most beautiful blossoms. Plenty of dogwoods grow wild in the woods, but they're never as beautiful as the ones growing in the yards of thoughtful owners who spray, fertilize, and manicure them in the early years. Trees, families, and friendships with good root systems cultivated over the course of years can weather storms with ease. In fact, they'll actually benefit from storms that harm or destroy others. The better they're cared for, the harder they are to kill. The more you apply these seven truths, the greater the hold you have on the hearts of the ones you love. A wife whose husband continually tends to her heart isn't likely to have it stolen by a better-looking male coworker. In fact, any attempted robbery will probably serve to drive her closer to her husband!

Sowing the right kind of seeds in the fertile ground of youth is the best way to build lifelong relationships with your children. But as children grow, the relationship must grow with them. We can't expect the fertilizer we put into the ground two years ago to keep having the same effect. If our garden is to keep growing, we'll have to apply more. It pains me to hear adult children talk about their parents like they're less than former acquaintances. Someone stopped sowing the right kind of seeds, and relied on old fertilizer to make what little they had planted grow.

Long-term application of these seven truths makes for long-term health in our relationships—but what if we have

OF DOGWOODS & DOGFIGHTS

neglected to do the right things for some time? Is it too late? Should we give up? Before I answer this, let me tell you two stories.

THE HISTORY OF O'HARE

I had flown through O'Hare International Airport in Chicago more times than I can count, without ever wondering how it came to be called O'Hare. As it turns out, the story of Butch O'Hare is well worth hearing.

Navy Lieutenant Commander Edward Henry (Butch) O'Hare was a World War II fighter pilot who had grown up in St. Louis, with frequent trips to Chicago where his father was in business. Having attended the U.S. Naval Academy, Butch was assigned to the Pacific fleet, where he flew one of eighteen Grumman F4F fighters assigned to the *USS Lexington*.

On February 20, 1942, nine Japanese bombers attacked the *Lexington*'s task force and were fought off by the carrier's pilots. While half the American planes landed on the carrier to refuel and the rest of the squadron pursued the Japanese survivors far into the distance, Butch and his wingman were the only combat-ready pilots in the air. At that moment, the *Lexington*'s radar detected a second wave of eight bombers only four minutes away, headed directly for the American fleet.

Butch and his wingman shot out to meet the enemy bombers, intending to take them together until more reinforcements could arrive. But all four machine guns on his wingman's fighter jammed, leaving only Butch and his payload of eighteen hundred bullets to defend the carrier and her screening ships against eight enemy bombers.

Fearlessly dropping down from above and behind the enemy formation, relying on instincts trained by thousands of hours of gunnery practice, Butch brought his single-engine Hellcat into point-blank range and scored hits on two of the enemy in his very first pass, forcing them out of formation. Without hesitation, he swept back around to hit the other side of the formation, braving the hail of enemy fire until he was close enough to see the Japanese pilots' horror as his .50-caliber M2 Brownings tore into their hulls. Down on the carrier's platform, the crews watched, wild with suspense, bursting into cheers as the lone fighter pilot scored hit after hit—at one point three flaming bombers could be seen falling simultaneously. Butch finally ran out of ammunition, but not before destroying three bombers outright and inflicting severe damage on three more. By this time more American fighters had joined the fray, pursuing the enemy away from the fleet. Only two Japanese planes ever made it back to their base.[1]

Sowing the right kind of seeds in the fertile ground of youth is the best way to build lifelong relationships with your children.

For his heroism, Butch O'Hare was awarded the Congressional Medal of Honor and became the first Navy

[1]Steve Ewing & John B. Lundstrom, "Four Minutes over the Lady Lex," in *Fateful Rendezvous: The Life of Butch O'Hare* (Annapolis: Naval Institute Press, 1997), 124-140.

Ace of World War II. President Franklin D. Roosevelt said of O'Hare that his was "one of the most daring, if not the most daring, single actions in the history of combat aviation." On November 26, 1943, while flying another combat mission, Butch was shot down and lost at sea. In 1949, two hundred thousand people turned out to witness the renaming of Chicago's Orchard Depot to O'Hare International Airport.

But what, you may be asking, does any of this have to do with building successful relationships?

THE REDEMPTION
OF A CROOKED LAWYER

Easy Eddie, as he was called, was an excellent lawyer and a successful businessman. His reputation was less than honorable, since his star client and business partner was none other than Alphonse (Al) Capone, perhaps America's best known and most feared criminal.

In his early days, Eddie made his money in dog racing, a business of questionable legality. Having convinced the wife of a deceased client to sell him the patent for the mechanical rabbit—the centerpiece of the dog racing enterprise—Eddie opened a track in Chicago, where the Mob's keen interest in dog racing as a low-overhead, high-profit business brought him into contact with Capone. It was the Prohibition Era; no business with a chance of turning a profit got off the ground without the blessing of the Mob. Soon Eddie and Al opened a string of dog tracks in various parts of the country. Eddie provided the business and financial skills that

Capone's organization needed to evade taxation on their less-than-legitimate money-making enterprises, and in return Capone loaned Eddie his political weight and capital.

But Eddie was also a doting father, and all his friends knew that he would do anything to secure the very best for his son. He sent him to the highly-regarded Western Military Academy school and wrote to contacts in Congress to secure him an appointment to West Point or Annapolis. But Eddie's son wasn't sold on the military, and Eddie feared that his son might be tempted instead to the easy money his father had made at racetracks—which, Eddie was beginning to realize, came with dark problems he never wanted his son to face. For the sake of his son, a change had to be made—somehow, a lifetime of poor choices needed to be redeemed.

In 1930, Eddie contacted federal prosecutors through a St. Louis reporter named John Rogers and offered to become an undercover source for the U.S. Treasury's investigation of Capone's organization. Eddie's insider knowledge and documentation of money transfers helped crack the federal case against Capone—and when Capone's men identified the members of the jury and tried to influence them, Eddie gave the prosecutors warning, allowing them to switch juries on the day of the trial and knock Capone's ace out of his hand. Capone was convicted in 1931 and spent the next eight years behind bars in Alcatraz.

Having worked with Capone for years, Eddie knew just what kind of man he had chosen to cross, and reports from other Alcatraz inmates that Capone was making threats against

Eddie couldn't have surprised him. On November 8, 1939, just after leaving his office in his new Lincoln coupe, Easy Eddie was gunned down in a mob-style execution. The assassins were never identified.

Twenty-seven months later, following in the steps of his father's heroism, Butch O'Hare plowed his fighter into the fray over the Gilbert Islands, saving the *USS Lexington*.[2] Butch O'Hare, you see, was Easy Eddie's son.

So, what if we have neglected to do the right things for some time? Is it too late? Should we give up?

ONE PROFOUND TRUTH, SEVEN APPLICATIONS

No one gets up in the morning hoping their relationships will fail. We all dream of growing old side by side with our spouse through the years. We all want our friendships to flourish, and our hearts long for our children to remain close to us forever. The trouble is that most people have no clue how to go about making this happen. They walk out into life with a hope and a prayer, letting the chips fall as they may; they have no idea how to intentionally build strong, lasting relationships. But not you. You know better.

You know that the heart is the centerpiece of life. And you know that whoever has the heart has the life! Your spouse

[2]Ewing and Lundstrom, "EJ Goes under Cover for the Treasury Department" and "The Sky Turned Black" in *Fateful Rendezvous*, 27-38 & 75-86.

is in love with whoever has their heart. Your friends spend time with whoever has their hearts. Your children follow whoever has their hearts. Your clients continually come back to whoever has their hearts. The secret to building the successful relationships of our dreams is winning and keeping the hearts of others.

Always remember: the most important things in life are the relationships that give life meaning. Seek to become an expert at unconditionally loving the people in your life. Look for ways to express faith in them. Develop the skill of being interested in the things that matter most to them. Make them a priority by being there when they need you. Everyone craves respect, so find ways to give it to them. Remember that your time is your life, and investing that time in people is key to opening their hearts. Never let the lifeline of communication become choked off—without it, no relationship can survive. Master these seven key principles, and you have mastered the art of winning and keeping hearts.

Make today count. Start now to develop new habits that will yield the richest of dividends in the areas that matter most—your relationships!

LOVE
Loving others without condition

• • •

FAITH
Believing more for someone
than they do for themselves

• • •

INTEREST
Valuing what others value

• • •

AVAILABILITY
Making room for others in crisis

• • •

RESPECT
Establishing a person's worth

• • •

TIME
The key to unlocking a heart

• • •

COMMUNICATION
The lifeline of every relationship

SOURCES

Britten, Terry & Graham Lyle. *What's Love Got to Do With It.* Capital Records, 1984.

Ewing, Steve & John B. Lundstrom. *Fateful Rendezvous: The Life of Butch O'Hare.* Annapolis: Naval Institute Press, 1997.

Lewis, C.S. *The Four Loves.* New York: Harcourt, Brace, 1960.

Merriam-Webster, s.v. "manipulation." Accessed April 12, 2016, http://www.merriam-webster.com/dictionary/manipulation.

"Raising Awareness About Sexual Abuse: Facts and Statistics." National Sex Offender Public Website, accessed April 12, 2016, https://www.nsopw.gov/en-US/Education/FactsStatistics?AspxAutoDetectCookieSupport=1#reference

ALSO BY MICHAEL FLETCHER

The Kingdom
A six-week study by Michael Fletcher with Jeff Christensen

An angel imposter: cloaked in darkness and armed with pride and greed. A coup: devastation prevails on the planet, and poisons the soul of man. A divine revolutionary: filled with power and light, armed with truth, clothed in humility. It's a story of violence and peace—of intrigue and romance—of revolution and redemption. It's a story as ancient as time itself...and this all-encompassing epic includes us all.

LifeGiving Marriage
A six-week study by Michael and Laura Fletcher

The design for marriage was formulated by God in the Garden of Eden...before sin came into the human race. God intended it to be an awe-inspiring, intimate, fruitful, joyous relationship—in short, life-giving! Marriage should be a source of joy to both husband and wife, and a source of strength, confidence, and encouragement to all the members of the family. This six-week study is designed to help us rediscover God's design for the LifeGiving Marriage.

Overcoming Barriers to Church Growth

Passionate about church growth, Michael Fletcher understands the obstacles pastors and church leaders face as they reach 100-200 and 700-800 member barriers. He lays out clear, practical steps churches can follow to achieve the growth they desire. His strategies have proved effective not only in his church, which has grown dramatically, but also across the nation.

HOW TO GET PROMOTED

If you want to get promoted, ask advice from the person who makes the decision! Michael sought the expert advice of 31 successful business leaders, entrepreneurs, pastors and military leaders—people who make and break careers. Their surprising insights, combined with the clear teaching of Scripture, make this book a must-read for anyone wanting to get ahead in life. Soundly biblical, unashamedly practical, and sometimes in-your-face, *How to Get Promoted* will prepare you to go to the next level!

BEYOND RECONCILIATION
with Larry Jackson

We hear many Christian leaders preaching the need for racial reconciliation in our country—but we don't see much real change taking place in our churches. Why do so few people experience true friendships with brothers or sisters of a different cultural background? Why are so few churches multi-ethnic? The fact is that the message of reconciliation is only the starting point. In sharing their own story of an extraordinary covenant friendship across cultural boundaries, Larry and Michael shed light on the perspectives, leadership, and initiative that can produce hope and lasting reconciliation.